What they said about the book...

'This handbook does a brilliant job o
secretary to life and dusting away the
explaining how this vital role can con.   ....,
organisation. If you are new to the sector or the role, it gives a
wonderful insight into the relevance of the role and how you can
make sure that your organisation is following good governance
practice. The author writes in a way that is easy to understand and
her knowledge and experience means that even seasoned secretaries
will be given new food for thought!'
Phillippa Caine, Association Secretary, Guide Dogs

'A practical, reliable and engaging guide for everyone in the role of
secretary to boards of charities or voluntary sector bodies. Read this
book and you, like its author, may fall in love with this great role and
these wonderful organisations!'
**Cecile Gillard, Legal Manager, Charities, Burton Sweet and Company
Secretarial Manager, Bates Wells Braithwaite**

'I have known the author for many years and this book is emblematic
of her personal approach to this vital role. The book is
comprehensive, thoughtful, easy to read and an incredibly useful tool
for anyone responsible for company secretarial matters. The advice
at the end of each chapter, as well as the checklists at the end of the
book, are an absolutely invaluable aid to anyone new to the role and
keen to get it right.'
**Richard Leaman-Grey CB OBE, Chief Executive Officer, Tall Ships
Youth Trust**

'Written by an active practitioner, this book provides an expert guide
on what the role of board secretary means in everyday practice. This
is not only for those who find themselves new to this role, but an
important reference tool for anyone who works on or reports to a
board.'
Jitinder Takhar, Chief Executive Officer, Local Space Ltd

KEY GUIDES

The Board Secretary's Handbook

Kirsty Semple

dsc
directory of social change

Published by the Directory of Social Change (Registered Charity no. 800517 in England and Wales)

Head office: Resource for London, 352 Holloway Road, London N7 6PA

Northern office: Suite 103, 1 Old Hall Street, Liverpool L3 9HG

Tel: 020 7697 4200

Visit www.dsc.org.uk to find out more about our books, subscription funding websites and training events. You can also sign up for e-newsletters so that you're always the first to hear about what's new.

The publisher welcomes suggestions and comments that will help to inform and improve future versions of this and all of our titles. Please give us your feedback by emailing publications@dsc.org.uk.

It should be understood that this publication is intended for guidance only and is not a substitute for professional or legal advice. No responsibility for loss occasioned as a result of any person acting or refraining from acting can be accepted by the authors or publisher.

First published 2018

Print ISBN 978 1 78482 009 1
Digital ISBN 978 1 78482 010 7

British Library Cataloguing in Publication Data
A catalogue record for this book is available from the British Library

Cover and text design by Kate Griffith
Typeset by Marlinzo Services, Frome
Printed and bound by Page Bros, Norwich

Contents

About the series

This series of key guides is designed for people involved with not-for-profit organisations of any size, no matter how you define your organisation – voluntary, community, non-governmental or social enterprise. All the titles offer practical, comprehensive, yet accessible advice to enable readers to get the most out of their roles and responsibilities.

There are several other titles available in this series; you can find details about the whole range at www.dsc.org.uk/key.

For further information, please contact DSC using the contact details as given in the following section, About the Directory of Social Change.

About the Directory of Social Change

The Directory of Social Change (DSC) has a vision of an independent voluntary sector at the heart of social change. We believe that the activities of independent charities, voluntary organisations and community groups are fundamental to achieve social change. We exist to help these organisations in achieving their goals.

We do this by:

- Providing practical tools that organisations and activists need, including online and printed publications, training courses and conferences on a huge range of topics

- Acting as a 'concerned citizen' in public policy debates, often on behalf of smaller charities, voluntary organisations and community groups

- Leading campaigns and stimulating debate on key policy issues that affect those groups

- Carrying out research and providing information to influence policymakers, as well as offering bespoke research for the voluntary sector

DSC is the leading provider of information and training for the voluntary sector and publishes an extensive range of guides and handbooks covering subjects such as fundraising, management, communication, finance and law. Our subscription-based websites contain a wealth of information on funding from grant-making charities, companies and government sources. We run more than 300 training courses each year, including bespoke in-house training provided at the client's location. DSC conferences and fairs, which take place throughout the year, also provide training on a wide range of topics and offer a welcome opportunity for networking.

For details of all our activities, and to order publications and book courses, go to www.dsc.org.uk, call 020 7697 4200 or email cs@dsc.org.uk.

About the author

Kirsty Semple ACIS LLM is a governance consultant and is Director of Semple Associates Ltd, formed in 2001. She is also editor of the *ICSA Charities Handbook*. Specialising in corporate governance and compliance, Kirsty has provided consultancy, training and support to boards of numerous voluntary sector organisations for 18 years. Before going into public practice, Kirsty was Company Secretary of the disability charity Scope. She now acts as secretary for a range of organisations, including the Born Free Foundation and the National Garden Scheme.

Acknowledgements

The author and publishers would like to thank Cecile Gillard, Joanne Saintclair-Abbott and Neal Green for their input at different stages of this book's preparation. Their knowledge, experience and insights have been invaluable.

Foreword

Welcome to the first edition of *The Board Secretary's Handbook*. As someone with a keen interest in good governance and a former board secretary myself, I am delighted to see this new title added to DSC's excellent catalogue of publications.

The House of Lords Select Committee on Charities has described the voluntary sector as 'the eyes, ears and conscience of society'.[1] I see the board secretary as the ears, eyes and conscience of their organisation. As well as this Committee, sector regulators are now more vocal about their expectations of voluntary sector organisations – they believe that the way they operate should give the public (whether as donors, users of services or as volunteers) confidence in what they are doing, and how they are going about it. Adopting a good governance code is seen as one way of helping to demonstrate this.

Within this context, the handbook's publication comes at a time when the regulatory and governance expectations of voluntary sector organisations are growing dramatically. Regulatory bodies are emphasising the need for board members to be assured that their individual organisations are complying with requirements, with a raft of new regulations having been introduced. It is therefore no surprise that these organisations are increasingly appointing board secretaries. They are instrumental in helping the organisation navigate their way through new regulatory landscapes and meeting good governance practice.

Whether a board secretary is paid or is a volunteer, they play a vital role in helping to ensure the integrity of the organisation's governance arrangements. They support the board in its decision-making and ensure statutory and regulatory compliance. In short, a board secretary helps glue the organisation together, providing a valuable source of knowledge along the way.

Every board secretary, from those new to the role through to seasoned professionals, will find this guide useful. It will help new board secretaries settle into their role and will make life easier for those who are more experienced, thanks to its tools, techniques and checklists. I commend this invaluable resource as essential reading for every board secretary.

Rosie Chapman FCIS, Chair, Charity Governance Code Steering Group

---

[1] *Stronger charities for a stronger society* [PDF], House of Lords Select Committee on Charities, Report of Session 2016–17, HL Paper 133, 2017, accessible at https://publications.parliament.uk/pa/ld201617/ldselect/ldchar/133/133.pdf, p. 3, accessed 7 August 2018.

Who this book is for

This book is written for 'you' as a current or prospective board secretary. Throughout, we tend to speak directly to you the board secretary rather than to the board of the organisation itself, or to staff, advisers or other readers who want to know about the role.

The book provides information for new board secretaries anywhere in the UK. The legal and regulatory requirements in this book are based on England and Wales. There are differences in law and regulation across the four nations of the UK, but the basic principles of good board secretarial skills apply throughout the UK, and apply to not-for-profit organisations, charities, co-operatives and and community interest companies.

Many of the basic principles also apply across the board, regardless of what legal form the organisation takes.

We use the words 'voluntary sector' as our terminology of choice to describe the sector as a whole. However, the term voluntary sector is all-encompassing, incorporating both organisations that are charities and those that are not. We use the terms 'charity' or 'charities' rather than voluntary sector where the context is specific to charities, such as in relation to legal requirements or where we have quoted information.

The term 'company secretary' is the most commonly used title for the role covered in this book, but many voluntary organisations are not companies. For the purposes of this book, we use the term 'board secretary' as nearly every organisation will have a board and one of the secretary's key roles is managing that board.

1 Why do you need a board secretary?

I have been a board secretary of voluntary organisations for 25 years, and I love it. I have been extremely lucky to have built a career out of it. I love working in the sector, and I love the role of secretary. I have found myself a role that suits my skills and my personality – but I am lucky. Like most people, I came into this role entirely by accident. I have to admit that I do a job that very few people aspire to; I have never come across a child who grew up wanting to be a board secretary! However, this is not primarily because most people do not *want* to do what I do; it is more that most people do not know what the role entails.

This fairly low level of understanding of the role extends across the voluntary, public and private sectors. But, while there are equivalents of board secretaries in all sectors, in my opinion it is in the voluntary sector that the role is most frequently unsung or misunderstood. The first time I ever got a job as a board secretary it was for a housing association, and the role was described as company secretary. I was so proud and so pleased. But I could not explain it to my mother – she thought that being a company secretary meant that I would be doing the typing for the whole company. This kind of misperception is partly to do with a lack of understanding of the official title of board secretary, but the nature of the role is still misunderstood when it is described through alternative titles, such as head of governance.

Let's be honest – if you are a board secretary for a voluntary organisation, the chances are you fell into the role or had it foisted upon you. It is quite rare for voluntary organisations to have a full-time professional secretary, but there is usually a perception that someone will need to take on the role. The board will often look around and find the best person it can. The role may be taken on by a board member or another volunteer, but often it is combined with another job. It is very common for the chief executive, or director of finance, to take on the role. It is also very common for people to walk into their new job and find out on their first day, through a comment or an aside, that they are expected to act as the board secretary.

So why does the role get imposed upon people? If there are very few people out there who want to be a board secretary, why does it exist as a role at all? How necessary is it?

When asking why an organisation should have a board secretary, it is probably best to start off by looking at what the role is. It differs from place to place but the key responsibilities of a board secretary include:

- ensuring the integrity of the governance framework;
- being responsible for supporting the board and managing its decision-making processes;
- ensuring compliance with statutory and regulatory requirements.

Sometimes the role is also described as being the chief administrative officer of an organisation, but this tends to suggest that the role is more operational than it is, so this description probably does not give a true assessment of the position.

Role title: board secretary

'Company secretary' is the most commonly used title for the role that is covered in this book, but many voluntary organisations are not companies. This means that other titles – such as 'clerk', 'charity secretary', 'foundation secretary' and 'honorary secretary' – are used. For the purposes of this book, the term 'board secretary' is always used, as in nearly every instance the organisation will have a board and one of the key roles of the secretary is to manage that board.

Having said that, while board secretary is one of the most generic terms, it is also one of the least frequently used. Chances are, if you are undertaking the role, you will be called something different, such as 'company secretary', 'secretary to the board' or 'association secretary'. It is also important to recognise that, because it is the most commonly understood description of the role, the term company secretary is very often used even if the organisation is not a company.

This book uses the term board secretary despite the fact that it is less commonly used, because it is the term that most types of secretary will understand applies to them.

In this book, where the term board secretary or secretary is used, it is intended to cover all people who may cover the role outlined. Where a more specific term is used, such as company secretary, society secretary or association secretary, what is being said applies specifically to that type of organisation and the role within it.

A note on capital letters in titles and other words

While it will be usual in your organisation's minutes, constitutions and other legal documents (such as contracts) to refer to the Board, the Chair, the Secretary and so on with capital letters, in a book dedicated to the subject these terms will all be used very frequently and the overuse of capital letters could become intrusive. As a result, this book does not use initial capitals for these terms except where it refers to an actual person's official title.

The general title or term secretary can refer to many different jobs – such as a personal assistant, a company secretary or the Secretary of State – but the word comes from the Latin word for secrets (*secernere*) and a secretary is essentially a keeper of secrets. There is a clear link here with the fact that a secretary is usually the person who keeps the records and minutes of an organisation. But why does an organisation need somebody to keep these records and to be the source of corporate knowledge in this way?

Is it a legal requirement?

The voluntary sector contains organisations which take many different forms. These will be looked at later in the book, but it is important to note that most of these legal forms do not have a statutory requirement to have a secretary. One of the legal forms used is the company, and until 2008 all companies were legally required to have a company secretary. The Companies Act 2006 changed this and now only public companies (those whose ownership is spread among the general public, usually through traded shares of stock) must have a secretary.[1] However, many other companies have chosen to retain a company secretary, particularly not-for-profit companies. Also, regardless of the legal requirements, the constitutions of many of these organisations refer to the role and make it a requirement. Where a constitution has such a requirement, this must be followed and the organisation cannot choose not to have a secretary unless it amends its constitution. Even if they are not required by the constitution, board secretaries are still commonly appointed.

When the core roles of the board secretary are examined, it is clear that all of these tasks have to be done by somebody, and so it makes sense to combine them into one role. Having a secretary also makes the governance of an organisation much easier. It frees up the chair's time, enabling them to better oversee board meetings, and it also frees up the chief executive's and other staff members' time, enabling them to better implement the decisions of the board.

It is often said that the secretary is the person who looks after an organisation; they are the person who holds the organisation together in terms of its governance. This might also explain why the role is so often found in the voluntary sector. By their very nature, voluntary organisations have boards comprising voluntary members. Many have

---

[1] 'Companies Act 2006' [web page], UK Government, 2006, www.legislation.gov.uk/ukpga/2006/46/section/270 and www.legislation.gov.uk/ukpga/2006/46/section/271, Sections 270(1) and 271, accessed 13 December 2017.

very few, if any, staff. Having one person who looks after the records, keeps a check on compliance and manages the governance processes for the organisation is crucial.

The board secretary can ensure that there is some form of continuity and that the history of how the organisation is being maintained does not get lost. Do you need to know who was on the board in 1972? The board secretary is the person to ask. Do you need to find a record of a decision taken by the board in 2002? Again, it is the board secretary whom you should ask. The board secretary also acts as the contact point for regulators and makes sure that the organisation is fulfilling its regulatory compliance requirements.

Many voluntary organisations are companies. While, as mentioned previously in this section, there is no longer a legal requirement for this kind of company to have a secretary, the Companies Act 2006 does make it clear that the functions of a secretary still need to be performed. It states that:

> Anything else required or authorised to be done by or to the secretary of the company may be done by or to—
> i) a director, or
> ii) a person authorised generally or specifically in that behalf by the directors.[2]

Of all the types of legal forms that not-for-profit organisations take, the only ones that are legally required to have a secretary are registered societies (co-operative and community benefit societies – see chapter 5, page 41). For example, the Co-operative and Community Benefit Societies Act 2014 states that every application for registration must be signed by the society's secretary.[3] In addition, any amendment of the society's rules must be signed by the secretary.

There is no legal requirement for a charitable incorporated organisation to have a secretary, and The Charitable Incorporated Organisations (General) Regulations 2012 makes no reference to the role.[4]

---

[2] 'Companies Act 2006' [web page], UK Government, 2006, www.legislation.gov.uk/ukpga/2006/46/section/270, Section 270(3)(b), accessed 13 December 2017.

[3] 'Co-operative and Community Benefit Societies Act 2014' [web page], UK Government, 2014, www.legislation.gov.uk/ukpga/2014/14/part/1, Part 1, accessed 13 December 2017.

[4] 'The Charitable Incorporated Organisations (General) Regulations 2012' [web page], UK Government, 2012, www.legislation.gov.uk/uksi/2012/3012/contents/made, accessed 13 December 2017.

Constitutional requirements

Regardless of whether there is a statutory requirement to have a secretary, an organisation generally has a legal requirement to meet the requirements of its constitution, and many constitutions include a requirement to have a secretary.

The Charity Commission's model articles of association (a model constitution for a charitable company) include references to a secretary, although these can be taken out.[5] The same is true of the Charity Law Association's model articles, but these are not free to access like the Charity Commission's model.[6] The UK government's own model articles for private companies limited by guarantee also refer to the role, although it is not listed as a requirement.[7] Model rules for registered societies will include references to the role, as it is a necessity in these types of organisation. Regardless of whether model constitutions have been used, it is a very common feature of constitutions across the voluntary sector to have a requirement for a board secretary. The structure of organisation that least commonly appoints board secretaries is trusts, although secretaries are still found here – sometimes under the title clerk to the trustees.

Outcomes and actions

After reading this chapter, you should understand:
- why organisations have a board secretary;
- why the term secretary is used;
- what the name secretary implies about the role.

It should be clear that whether it is a requirement for your organisation to have a secretary or not depends on your organisation's legal form and the wording in its constitution. However, even if it is not a requirement, somebody will still need to do the core work of a secretary.

---

[5] *Charitable Companies: Model articles of association* [PDF], Charity Commission, 2017, www.gov.uk/government/uploads/system/uploads/attachment_data/file/586363/GD1_articles_of_association.pdf, accessed 13 December 2017.

[6] *Memorandum and Articles of Association*, 3rd edition, Gillingham, Charity Law Association, 2017.

[7] 'Model articles of association for limited companies' [web page], Companies House, 2014, www.gov.uk/guidance/model-articles-of-association-for-limited-companies, accessed 13 December 2017.

2 Roles, duties and responsibilities

The secretary will usually be responsible for:
- organising the meetings of the board;
- organising any committees and general meetings of the organisation;
- ensuring that there is a process for the appointment of board members and that they are appointed in accordance with the constitution;
- ensuring that the organisation is well governed;
- keeping the records of the organisation;
- ensuring compliance with legislative and regulatory requirements;
- looking after the constitution of the organisation.

The work involved in organising meetings of the board is quite varied. It includes:
- calling the meetings;
- drafting the agenda (along with the chair);
- sending out the agenda and papers to board members;
- overseeing the administration of the meeting, such as booking the venue;
- checking who will be attending and in what capacity;
- being responsible for the minutes and checking on follow-up actions.

Ensuring that the organisation is well governed is sometimes just about ensuring that the board is working to the correct processes – and that those processes are effective and not a hindrance. However, sometimes it is a much broader role, and to perform this role a secretary needs to keep up to date with governance best practice across the sector. To properly look after the constitution, the secretary needs to understand it, advise the board of its contents and deal with any amendments.

The secretary is also often the person who looks after legal matters for the organisation. The role is sometimes assigned to someone who has a legal background, in which case they may themselves be the source of legal advice. If not, they may still be the person who deals with the provision of legal advice to the organisation – in other words, the person who instructs solicitors. They are also often the central point for dealing with contracts, including reviewing them and getting them signed. Even if you do not have a legal background, as a secretary you should quickly gain an oversight of the law that applies to your organisation (such as charity law or company law) sufficient to understand its requirements and provide some basic advice.

The secretary is often the person who is responsible for data protection in a voluntary organisation. There is legislation that protects how organisations hold and process personal data, meaning information about individuals. As secretary, you need to be aware of the legal requirements in regard to the personal data that you hold, such as what is recorded in minutes and the information that you hold in records and registers. You may also be responsible for overseeing data protection across the organisation. The legal requirements regarding data protection are beyond the scope of this book, but if you are responsible for data protection you should ensure that this is clearly specified in your role description and that you have the necessary training and resources to carry out the role. If you are named as Data Protection Officer for your organisation, you should also be aware that the General Data Protection Regulation (Regulation (EU) 2016/679) sets out certain rights and tasks for Data Protection Officers.

Model role description: board secretary

This role description applies to the secretary of a charitable company. For a different type of organisation, it would need to be adapted accordingly.

Key purpose

To take the lead on the compliance and governance of the organisation, making sure that appropriate governance structures and processes are in place and working effectively to enable the board to discharge its responsibilities as the governing body.

General responsibilities

1 Facilitating the smooth operation of the company's formal decision-making and reporting machinery, including:
- organising board meetings;
- organising committee meetings;
- organising and recording decisions taken by written resolution;
- ensuring committees are constituted in compliance with the articles, are provided with clear terms of reference, and regularly have their membership reviewed and refreshed;
- formulating meeting agendas for the board and committees with the chair (and the chief executive if applicable);
- advising on the content and organisation of papers for meeting agendas;
- overseeing the collection, organisation and distribution of such information, documents or other papers required for the meetings;
- ensuring that minutes are taken for all board and committee meetings, that the minute books are maintained and that certified copies of the minutes are kept;

- keeping a log of matters arising in meetings and the actions taken on them;
- assisting the chair in ensuring that meetings are as effective as possible.

2   Ensuring that general meetings are held in accordance with the requirements of the Companies Act 2006 and the articles, including:

- obtaining board agreement to all documentation for circulation to members;
- overseeing the preparation and issuing of notices of meetings and the distribution of proxy forms;
- ensuring that proxy forms are correctly processed and that voting is carried out accurately;
- co-ordinating the administration of meetings and ensuring that appropriate minutes are kept.

3   Ensuring that the organisation complies with its articles, and drafting and incorporating amendments in accordance with correct procedures.

4   Maintaining the following registers:

- company charges;
- directors and secretary;
- directors' residential addresses;
- members.

5   Filing information with the Charity Commission and Registrar of Companies to report certain changes regarding the company or to comply with requirements for periodic filing, including annual returns and confirmation statements. Additionally, filing the annual report and accounts.

6   Continually reviewing developments in corporate governance and helping to ensure that the charity's own governance framework and processes are as effective as possible.

7   Advising and assisting the board members with respect to their duties and responsibilities, in particular regarding compliance with charity and company law.

8   Facilitating good information flows between board members and acting as a channel of communication and information for board members.

9   Advising on ensuring that all business letters, notices and other official publications of the charity show the name of the charity and any other information as required by law and that charity nameplates are displayed in a conspicuous place.

10   Establishing a summary of matters reserved for decision by the board, a scheme of delegation and so on.

11   Maintaining records of board members' appointments and ensuring that terms of office, appointments and re-appointments are handled appropriately.

12   Establishing and communicating procedures for board members to take independent professional advice at the company's expense if required.

13   Advising on probity issues in regard to the board, including overseeing the mechanisms for dealing with conflicts of interest.

14   Liaising with the finance manager on the publication and distribution of the company's annual report and accounts and, in particular, advising on the preparation of the board members' report.

Authority and liability

What authority does a board secretary have?

If the board secretary is an employee, or if the board has agreed a role description, this usually gives the secretary authority to act for the organisation in certain situations. Aside from that, it has also been maintained in the courts that a company secretary has ostensible authority in a company. There was a legal case in 1971 in which the courts established that a car hire firm was entitled to rely on the secretary's ostensible authority as the company's chief administrative officer.[1] In this case, the company secretary hired cars in the name of the company that were in fact for his own private use. The company refused to pay for the hire, saying that it was not bound by the hire contracts, as the secretary did not have the authority to enter into them. The matter went to court and the car hire company won. Lord Denning, the judge, wrote:

> [A company secretary] is an officer of the company with extensive duties and responsibilities. This appears not only in the modern Companies Acts, but also by the role which he plays in the day-to-day business of companies. He is no longer a mere clerk. He regularly makes representations on behalf of the company and enters into contracts on its behalf which come within the day-to-day running of the company's business. So much so that he may be regarded as held out as having authority to do such things on behalf of the company. He is certainly entitled to sign contracts connected with the administrative side of a company's affairs, such as employing staff, and ordering cars, and so forth. All such matters now come within the ostensible authority of a company's secretary.[2]

In addition to this common-law authority to act, you should also note that a company secretary has the power to act as a co-signatory for entering into deeds on behalf of a company (along with a director).[3]

In a company, the secretary can file documents on behalf of the company. The forms used by Companies House state that they can be signed and/or submitted by a director or secretary, or by an authorised person if there is

---

[1] Panorama Developments (Guildford) Ltd v Fidelis Furnishing Fabrics Ltd (1971), 2 QB, 711.

[2] Panorama Developments (Guildford) Ltd v Fidelis Furnishing Fabrics Ltd (1971), 2 QB, 711 at 716–717.

[3] 'Companies Act 2006' [web page], UK Government, 2006, www.legislation.gov.uk/ukpga/2006/46/section/44, Section 44(3)(b), accessed 13 December 2017.

no secretary.[4] In a registered society, the secretary must sign applications for registration and for changes to the rules.[5]

It is also often the secretary who verifies documents on behalf of the organisation, such as copies of the constitution, or statements of resolutions and minutes. From time to time you may be asked to provide a certified copy of a document. Certifying a document is confirming that it is a true copy. There are no set legal rules on certifying documents – the procedure depends on the requirements of the organisation seeking the certification. However, while some parties require the signature of a solicitor on certifications, in the case of documents relating to a company, a director or secretary of that company is often considered to be able to make a certification. If you are the secretary and have a professional qualification that relates to this role – for example, if you are a member of the Institute of Chartered Secretaries and Administrators (ICSA: The Governance Institute) or are a qualified accountant – this will provide further evidence that you can be trusted to make a certification.

What liabilities does a board secretary have?

A board secretary does not have legal duties in the same way that a company director or charity trustee does, but the role does carry some liabilities. The Companies Act 2006 includes company secretaries in the definition of officers; it states that 'officer, in relation to a body corporate, includes a director, manager or secretary'.[6] This means that being the secretary of a company does carry some liabilities. Under the Companies Act 2006, if the Act is breached 'an offence is committed by every officer of the company who is in default', which would include the secretary.[7] Such defaults could include a failure to file a change in the details of the company's directors and secretary or a failure to file the company's confirmation statement. However, it should be noted that, in practice, relevant authorities (such as Companies House) usually focus on the

---

[4] 'Companies Act 2006' [web page], UK Government, 2006, www.legislation.gov.uk/ukpga/2006/46/section/274, Section 274, accessed 17 May 2018.

[5] 'Co-operative and Community Benefit Societies Act 2014' [web page], UK Government, 2014, www.legislation.gov.uk/ukpga/2014/14/contents, Section 3(1)(a)(i) and Section 16(2), accessed 13 December 2017.

[6] 'Companies Act 2006' [web page], UK Government, 2006, www.legislation.gov.uk/ukpga/2006/46/section/1173, Section 1173, accessed 13 December 2017.

[7] 'Companies Act 2006' [web page], UK Government, 2006, www.legislation.gov.uk/ukpga/2006/46/section/1121, Section 1121, accessed 13 December 2017.

directors rather than the secretary in relation to statutory compliance defaults.

It can also be argued that if a board secretary is considered to be an officer of an organisation, and particularly if that organisation is a company, this means that they owe a legal duty to act in good faith and in the best interests of the company, and that a breach of this duty could potentially result in the secretary becoming liable to the company for damages. This is what is called a fiduciary duty. This can be seen in the statement of the judge in the aforementioned case concerning a car hire firm.[8] He spoke of a company secretary being an 'officer of the company with extensive duties and responsibilities', meaning this fiduciary duty. This means that it is advisable for a board secretary to declare any conflict of interest, avoid them in the same way that a board member should, and not receive secret profits (see chapter 5, page 48).

In the same way that a company secretary is an officer (and liable for breaches of the Companies Act 2006), a registered society's secretary is also an officer and can be held liable for breaches.

Can anybody be appointed as a board secretary?

Public companies, which have their shares listed on the stock exchange, have particular requirements regarding the types of qualification that their secretaries must have. But no voluntary organisation is one of these types of company, even if it is a company. Voluntary organisations are called 'private companies', which means these rules do not apply to them. If your organisation is a company, there are a few restrictions as to who can be a company secretary. Specifically, a company's auditors cannot act as its company secretary and a company secretary must not be an undischarged bankrupt unless given leave by the court. None of the other legal forms place restrictions on who can act as a board secretary, but you should bear in mind the notes in this section regarding the fit and proper persons test for charities.

However, there is also a restriction on companies where somebody acts as both a director and a secretary. While a person can take on both roles, they cannot act in a dual capacity. The Companies Act 2006 states:

> A provision requiring or authorising a thing to be done by or to a director and the secretary of a company is not satisfied by its being done by or to

---

[8] Panorama Developments (Guildford) Ltd v Fidelis Furnishing Fabrics Ltd (1971).

the same person acting both as director and as, or in place of, the secretary.[9]

While there are not any general disqualifications that apply to the role, you will need to take some care if your organisation is a charity. HMRC applies a 'fit and proper persons test' to community amateur sports clubs and charities. This requirement was introduced by the Finance Act 2010.[10] The Act introduced a definition of charity for tax purposes that includes a management condition. For a charity to satisfy the management condition, its managers must be 'fit and proper' persons.[11] The test applies to the managers of the charity and not just its trustees. The term 'manager' is defined in the legislation as 'the persons having the general control and management of the administration of the body or trust'.[12]

The term 'general control and management' has a wider scope than in the Charities Act 2011. HMRC in its own guidance states that, 'for example, in a typical small local charity a manager could include the Chairperson, Treasurer, Secretary and the rest of the management committee who have control over expenditure'.[13] In this instance, the term 'management committee' means the same thing as 'board'. The sorts of things that may lead HMRC to conclude that a person is not fit and proper include (but are not limited to):

• having been involved in tax fraud;
• having been involved in other fraudulent behaviour, including misrepresentation and/or identity theft;
• having been involved in attacks against, or abuse of, tax repayment systems;
• having used a tax avoidance scheme featuring charitable reliefs or using a charity to facilitate the avoidance;

---

[9] 'Companies Act 2006' [web page], UK Government, 2006, www.legislation.gov.uk/ukpga/2006/46/section/280, c. 46, Part 12, Section 280, accessed 27 March 2018.

[10] 'Finance Act 2010' [web page], UK Government, 2010, www.legislation.gov.uk/ukpga/2010/13/contents, accessed 13 December 2017.

[11] 'Finance Act 2010' [web page], UK Government, 2010, www.legislation.gov.uk/ukpga/2010/13/schedule/6/paragraph/4, Schedule 6, Part 1, Para 4 (1), accessed 13 December 2017.

[12] 'Finance Act 2010' [web page], UK Government, 2010, www.legislation.gov.uk/ukpga/2010/13/schedule/6/paragraph/4, Schedule 6, Part 1, Para 4 (2), accessed 13 December 2017.

[13] 'Guidance on the fit and proper persons test' [web page], HM Revenue & Customs, 2017, www.gov.uk/government/publications/charities-fit-and-proper-persons-test/guidance-on-the-fit-and-proper-persons-test, accessed 13 December 2017.

- having been involved in designing and/or promoting tax avoidance schemes;
- being an undischarged bankrupt;
- having made an arrangement with creditors that is still undischarged;
- having been barred from acting as a charity trustee by a charity regulator or court;
- having been disqualified from acting as a company director.

HMRC provides a help sheet and model declaration for fit and proper persons.[14] If your organisation is a charity, you should already be using this, or a similar declaration, for your trustees. A board secretary of a charity should also be asked to fill out this declaration, and care should be taken that nothing applies that could lead to the board secretary not being considered fit and proper.

Core competencies of the board secretary

If you are looking to appoint a board secretary, it is a good idea to think about the key characteristics of a good board secretary. If you are appointing somebody in a paid, professional capacity, you will want them to have the right skills, as set out in the next bulleted list. However, you may not have the possibility of bringing somebody in with this skill set. If you yourself have been asked to take on the role, you will want to consider whether you would be suitable for it.

A very good document to look at when considering the skills and competencies needed is *The Company Secretary: Building trust through governance*.[15] This document focuses on the role of company secretary. While the research was primarily undertaken in the commercial sector, many of its conclusions are transferable to the voluntary sector. If nothing else, if you have been newly appointed to the role and it seems rather dull and administrative, this document may give you a much better insight into how important and interesting the role is. You can also see from this research that, while technical skills are important, equally important are

---

[14] *Fit and proper persons helpsheet and declaration* [PDF], HMRC, 2018, https://assets.publishing.service.gov.uk/government/uploads/system/uploads/attachment_data/file/597664/Fit-and-proper-persons-helpsheet-and-declaration.pdf, accessed 6 June 2018.

[15] Andrew Kakabadse, Nada Korac-Kakabadse and Nadeem Khan, *The Company Secretary: Building trust through governance*, London, ICSA: The Governance Institute, 2014. (Accessible to ICSA members at www.icsa.org.uk/knowledge/research/the-company-secretary-report; accessible to non-members at www.geniusmethods.com/wp-content/uploads/2015/01/icsa-the-company-secretary-report.pdf.)

the characteristics of a secretary and the approach the secretary must take.

You will be able to develop technical skills in the role, if necessary. But you also need to consider the role's core competencies or, in other words, its key characteristics. The key characteristics of a good secretary can be summarised as:

- being well organised and task focused;
- having good analytical skills, the ability to evaluate a range of materials and the ability to form a judgement;
- possessing problem-solving skills in the sense of enjoying facing challenges and assessing ways of dealing with them;
- having discretion and a respect for confidential information;
- being able to retain a calm approach;
- having good communication skills and an ability to explain things clearly;
- being meticulous and having very good attention to detail – caring about the processes and the small stuff (a good board secretary will never think that the ends justify the means; they will always want to ensure that things are done in the right way);
- being independent and able to hold your own.

You may be considering whether the role would be a good one for you, but it can be quite difficult to assess whether you have these competencies. For example, a person might think of themselves as being rather disorganised, but other people may have a very different impression. Talk to somebody who knows you well. Show them the aforementioned list and seek their views on whether you might be right for the role. Also, try to work through the list and think of practical examples of when you have demonstrated each of these characteristics. Are these recent examples? Did they come easily to you? Are you able to think of more than one or two examples?

Another way of thinking about it is to consider some of the characteristics of somebody who would *not* be the best person for the job. Following are three different scenarios; imagine yourself in each. Do you think you would find it possible to act as a board secretary should in each scenario? It would be unusual to find all of these scenarios easy to deal with. But, if you put yourself into each scenario and determine in all three that you would not find it possible to act as a secretary should, being a board secretary is probably not the right choice for you.

Scenario 1

Imagine that you have recently been appointed as the board secretary of a local animal rescue service. The position is voluntary and the board secretary is not a board member. The board secretary attends the board meetings to take the minutes and to advise the board on any governance matters. You took on the role because you feel so passionately about the services that the organisation provides. The board is having a big strategic review and you are taking minutes of the discussions. As a result of these discussions, the board is leaning towards taking decisions that you think are fundamentally wrong for the organisation. You have no governance or compliance concerns with these decisions; you just fundamentally disagree with them. How do you think that you should react at the board meeting?

As the board secretary, and someone who is not a board member, your role at the meeting is to take the minutes and advise on governance matters. There are no governance issues arising in these decisions and so you should have no part in the decision-making. Sometimes, the board may invite others involved in the organisation to contribute their views, but it is for the board to choose to do this. Also, if you are asked, giving a view is different from trying to win the board members over to your point of view. In some instances, the board may have missed some key piece of information that you know about. It may be helpful for you to pass on that information. But you must take real care to distinguish between matters that are genuine gaps in the board's knowledge and matters where you are trying to influence the board's decision.

The board secretary usually attends board meetings, but they rarely speak. I sometimes say that a good meeting is one where the secretary never speaks, as this should mean that the board was able to take all its decisions without needing the secretary's advice.

Would you find it very difficult to hold back in this kind of discussion? Sometimes it is easier to be the board secretary for an organisation that you care about but where you do not have passionate views. A board secretary contributes to the strategy of an organisation, but only in the sense of managing the processes. If you are very focused on being able to set the strategic direction of an organisation, you are probably better waiting for a vacancy on its board and not being the board secretary.

Scenario 2

Imagine that you are the personal assistant to the chief executive of a small charity and have been asked to take on the role of board secretary. You minute the meetings of the board, and you submit the minutes to the chief executive and the chair before they go to board members.

At the previous meeting, you recorded a decision that your boss, the chief executive and the chair did not like. When you gave the draft minutes to them, they amended this section of your minutes to record the decision in a way that they preferred. It now reads very differently from the decision that was taken as stated in your notes.

How would you deal with this? Would you be able to challenge the chief executive (your manager) and the chair? Could you do this in a way that would be non-confrontational but where you would still hold your ground? Would your instinct be to just let it go, thinking that they are both important people in the organisation and so it is probably easier to just go along with them?

A board secretary needs to have sufficient resilience and independence to hold their ground on these matters. However, they also need good interpersonal skills to be able to manage situations like this as diplomatically as possible.

In such a situation, I would expect the secretary to first check back in their notes to confirm that they were correct. Sometimes we can get things wrong or minute in a way that reflects our own biases. The secretary should then go back to the chief executive and chair and explain why the minute was drafted as it originally was. They should be able to use their own notes on the meeting to back this up. If possible, they should find a way of resolving the disagreement. For example, could the minute be re-drafted in such a way as to still be accurate but to allay the chief executive and chair's concerns? If they both continued to say that they wanted their draft to go forward, then I would expect the secretary to say that when it came to agreeing the minutes at the next meeting, they would inform the other board members of the differing views on the proposed wording and ask them to determine which wording should be used. If, when this happened, the board agreed with the chair and chief executive, the secretary would accept the decision and move on, perhaps also taking minutes covering that discussion.

Could you do this? Or would you back down? Or, alternatively, might you find it really hard to let the matter go if the board backed the chair and chief executive?

Scenario 3

Imagine that you are the board secretary of a charity that provides counselling and support for people who are caring for those with dementia. The website of the charity states that 'we care for those who care' and talks of providing support for people in Yorkshire. However, the charity is in fact based in North Yorkshire, and you know that the purposes of the charity, as set out in its constitution, state that it will provide counselling and support in North Yorkshire. You do not think that anyone else has read the constitution. The charity has an opportunity to enter into a contract to provide services to an existing counselling body. That body is currently providing services just over the border in South Yorkshire, but all of its operations will be moving to North Yorkshire within the next three months. The board is very keen to enter into the contract now, or it may lose this opportunity. This would mean acting outside the charity's purposes initially, but the matter would be resolved within three months, and it is very unlikely that anybody would notice.

How would you advise the board? Would you draw the board's attention to the purposes clause? Would your instinctive feeling be that this is something best left alone and that it is essentially a bureaucratic nicety that does not really matter?

The reality is that, as the board secretary, you must draw the board's attention to any restriction that is placed on the charity by its objects. Entering into this contract at this time is potentially an *ultra vires* act, meaning one that is outside the powers of the charity. This has implications for the validity of the contract and also potentially places the board members in breach of their legal duties. They need to know all of this before deciding to act. If they decide to proceed, that is their decision, but they will do so knowingly and understanding the risks. The secretary should also advise the board on what the alternatives are. Could the purposes be amended, and how quickly? Could the start date for the contract be delayed?

If you feel very strongly that this restriction is best left alone and that the board secretary is potentially taking opportunities away from the charity, the role is probably not for you.

If you take on the role and have no background secretarial or legal knowledge, there are a number of ways that you can develop the necessary skills:

- **Reading:** This book is a start, but there is a wide range of reading materials out there. A reading list is included on page 203.
- **Courses:** There are a number of courses available. Look at courses provided by ICSA: The Governance Institute, the Directory of Social Change and the National Council for Voluntary Organisations (which offers online training). As well as courses on the secretary role, you may also consider some courses on specific skills, such as taking minutes.
- **Qualifications:** If you decide that this is work that you would like to take further, you could think about a qualification. ICSA: The Governance Institute is the best place to start. As well as its Chartered Secretaries Qualifying Scheme, it has a number of accredited postgraduate qualifications. It also has a Charity Law and Governance certificate and a Charity Management diploma.
- **Networking:** Take all of the opportunities you can to meet with and share information with people who provide a board secretary role in similar organisations. You may find that there is a professional group specific to your type of organisation. For example, there is a group specifically for the secretaries of housing associations: the National Housing Federation Governance Forum. Also, if you work for a charity, be aware that membership of the Charity Law Association is not restricted to lawyers. If you cannot find a group, consider setting one up.

- **Stay in touch:** Keep up to date with changes in the governance of the sector and legal matters. A number of the larger law firms that work in the sector provide regular newsletters to which you can subscribe. If your organisation is a charity, you should make sure that you receive the Charity Commission's quarterly newsletter.

Outcomes and actions

After reading this chapter, you should understand:
- the core roles of the secretary and the work secretaries are often asked to do;
- what authority the role has;
- what the liabilities of the role are;
- what the core competencies of the role are;
- what makes somebody a good secretary.

If you do not currently have a role profile or job description, you could use the information provided in this chapter to draft one. Reviewing the core competencies can also give you a better insight into whether the role is right for you.

3 Appointment of the board secretary

The board secretary reports to the board and so usually needs to be appointed by the board. An organisation's constitution will usually state that the board will appoint the secretary. This is not invariably the case; you may work for an organisation where the constitution states that you are appointed by the membership, particularly if you are also a board member. If you are an employee of the organisation, and being the board secretary is part of your role and is listed in your job description, this could be taken as implying your appointment, especially if the board agreed to the job description. However, unless the board has very clearly delegated the appointment of the secretary and the constitution allows it to do this, it would be advisable for the appointment to also be separately recorded by the board. This way, there would be absolute clarity that you were authorised to act. The minutes of the appointment should be kept. Typical wording is: 'It was agreed that [insert name here] be appointed as Board Secretary with immediate effect/with effect from [date].'

If having a board secretary is a requirement for your organisation, there should not be gaps between appointments. A new secretary's appointment should take effect when the previous board secretary steps down. If a new person has not yet been appointed, an interim appointment can be made.

It is very important that you remember the need to be formally appointed in this way, and make sure that it does happen. In many voluntary organisations, the role is likely to be combined with another role. The board may not have appointed you to that other role (you may have been appointed by the chief executive or another manager). However, if you are also expected to act as board secretary, you should ask that your appointment to that role be confirmed at the next board meeting.

Once the secretary is formally appointed, the appointment will need to be recorded in whatever registers and records the organisation holds. If the organisation is a company, the secretary's name and details will also need to be added to the register of secretaries (see chapter 13, page 138). If your organisation is a company and it chooses to have a company secretary, it must notify Companies House of the appointment within 14 days by submitting form AP03, titled 'Appoint a secretary'.[1] This can be done online or by post.

Organisations that are companies can appoint corporate bodies to act as the company secretary. In this way, if a firm of chartered secretaries was appointed to act on an outsourced basis, you could appoint the firm and not the individual employed by it. In such cases, there is a slightly different form for notifying Companies House: form AP04, titled 'Appoint a corporate secretary'.[2] There is no general reason why other types of organisation cannot also appoint a corporate body, but you should check your constitution to ensure that this is not prohibited before doing so.

Linked to the need to be appointed by the board is the fact that the board secretary should also report directly to the board. The secretary is responsible for the administration of board meetings as well as for the governance and compliance of the organisation. Therefore, they need to be able to communicate directly with the board on these matters. Even if the secretary is a member of staff with another role, the reporting of board secretarial matters should be direct to the board. If, for example, you are a head of finance who is also acting as board secretary, you may be reporting to the chief executive for your finance role. However, when it comes to acting as the board secretary, you should report to the board. This may mean that there are times when your advice to the board will contradict the advice of your manager. You will need to be prepared for this yourself and ensure that your manager is prepared too.

It is often difficult to negotiate a path through dual reporting, but you should put time and effort into making it work. For example, if you are asked to take on the board secretary role, you should make contact with the board's chair and arrange to meet to discuss how you will work together and how you will provide services for the board. Try to schedule these meetings on a regular basis.

If you are asked to take on the role of board secretary but not given the information and access that are necessary for the role, you should be aware that this means that you will not be able to fully perform the role. For example, a board secretary may not necessarily attend every board meeting (when the role is outsourced, the servicing of board meetings may still be undertaken by a member of staff), but they should have a clear

---

[1] 'Appoint a secretary (AP03)' [web page], Companies House, 2016, www.gov.uk/government/publications/appoint-a-secretary-ap03, accessed 13 December 2017.

[2] 'Appoint a corporate secretary (AP04)' [web page], Companies House, 2016, www.gov.uk/government/publications/appoint-a-corporate-secretary-ap04, accessed 13 December 2017.

right to attend such meetings, have access to board members, and be supplied with the board papers so that they can review them and advise the board accordingly.

Because the duties of the board secretary can differ from organisation to organisation, the board should have a clear understanding of what it is that they are asking the board secretary to do. The duties and responsibilities should be determined by the board and they should always be recorded in writing, preferably in a role description.

Joint and deputy board secretaries

Using the term 'the secretary' seems to clearly imply that there is only one secretary. However, organisations can usually appoint more than one secretary if they wish. Have a look in your organisation's constitution to see whether it says the role must only be held by one person. In many instances, it may be a good idea to think about having a joint secretary or a deputy secretary. Sometimes, a person will have the title of secretary – such as a board member who is an honorary secretary or a chief executive who also holds the post of board secretary – but somebody else undertakes all of the administrative duties, such as filing updates at the Charity Commission or Companies House. This person is effectively acting as a deputy secretary. Other times, it may be useful to have more than one person fulfilling the role. Your organisation may have a professional who provides the service on an outsourced basis but is not located close to the office and so is not always available to sign things off as secretary (such as changes in bank mandates). With this in mind, it might be useful to have somebody who is based in the office also appointed as secretary to sign such documents.

It is therefore perfectly permissible to have more than one secretary, but it is important to take care to make sure that it is clear how this will work and what authority each person has.

If your organisation is a company, you will need to pay attention to the Companies Act 2006, which refers to the appointment of deputy or assistant secretaries. It states:

> Where in the case of any company the office of secretary is vacant, or there is for any other reason no secretary capable of acting, anything required or authorised to be done by or to the secretary may be done— by or to an assistant or deputy secretary (if any).[3]

---

[3] 'Companies Act 2006' [web page], UK Government, 2006, www.legislation.gov. uk/ukpga/2006/46/section/274, Section 274, accessed 13 December 2017.

When the appointment of a joint or deputy secretary is recorded in the minutes, the wording must make it clear how the appointments will work. For example, if you are appointing joint secretaries, do not just call them that in the minutes – make it clear that they can act independently of each other. Otherwise it could be assumed that the joint secretaries will need to act jointly, meaning a document that must be signed by the secretary will need to be signed by both of them.

Model wording for minutes: appointment

Secretary

That, with effect from [*insert date*], XY be appointed as secretary of [*insert name of organisation*] and therefore have the authority to undertake the usual duties of, and exercise the usual powers conferred on, the secretary of [*insert name of organisation*].

Deputy secretary

That, with effect from [*insert date*], XY be appointed as deputy/assistant secretary of [*insert name of organisation*] with authority to undertake the duties of, and exercise the powers conferred on, the secretary of [*insert name of organisation*] when the secretary is incapable of acting in that capacity [*because of his/her absence from the office*].

Joint secretary

That, with effect from [*insert date*], AB and XY be appointed as joint secretaries of [*insert name of organisation*]. Both AB and XY are hereby granted authority to undertake the duties of, and exercise the powers conferred on, the role of secretary on their own and independently of the other.

If joint or deputy secretaries are appointed, the appointment of each should be entered on the register of secretaries (if such a register is held by the organisation) and notified to Companies House (if the organisation is a company). Registers must be held by certain types of organisations, such as companies. In notifying Companies House, there is no need to record the appointee as being a deputy or joint secretary. You will just complete the usual appointment form for a secretary (form AP03 or form AP04) or file the appointment online. The records will then show both appointees as secretary.

Ceasing to be board secretary

If a board secretary resigns, this should be reported to the board members immediately. If having a secretary is a legal or constitutional requirement, whenever possible boards should not allow a gap before a new appointment is made, even if this means appointing an interim secretary until a permanent replacement can be made. Therefore, resignations should, whenever possible, coincide with a board meeting, which can then also appoint the next secretary.

The board itself can also usually remove a board secretary, although you should check whether your constitution allows this. If the board secretary is also an employee, while the board may have the right to remove the person, this is likely to have wider contractual implications. As with appointments, removal of a board secretary should be taken down in the minutes (along with resignations).

It is important to note that only the board can remove a board secretary, and this role is distinct from your role or position as an employee or contractor. In this way, if you are employed and you are dismissed by the chief executive, or your role description is changed to remove you from the task of acting as secretary, the board must still also formally remove you unless you choose to resign or your appointment was ex officio (i.e. held explicitly by virtue of your other role). In addition, if you are contracted to undertake the role of secretary, the ending of that contract does not remove you; you can only be removed by the board or via your resignation. The only exception is where your appointment was for a time-limited term.

In the case of companies, resignation or removal must be notified to Companies House and details of the resignation or removal should be entered in the register of directors and secretaries.

Outcomes and actions

After reading this chapter, you should be clear about the appointment process. It might be wise for you to check back and make sure that you have been appointed in the appropriate way. Check that your appointment has been confirmed and that (if your organisation is a company) Companies House has been notified. You may also want to consider whether the appointment of a joint or deputy secretary would be appropriate for your organisation.

4 Other ways of working

The previous chapters have established that, other than for registered societies, there is no legal requirement to have a board secretary. Although it is a very useful way of working, it may be worth taking some time to consider alternatives.

Outsourced secretarial services

One option is to keep the role but get somebody else to do it. There are a number of organisations (and individuals) that provide outsourced secretarial services. If you are looking into this option, there are some important considerations for you to make before you go down this route. The three main options are as follows.

Chartered secretaries

Chartered secretaries are members of ICSA: The Governance Institute. This is the primary qualification for company secretaries, and the institute's members are familiar with a range of governance and compliance matters (the institute's qualifications include law and finance). There are a number of members in public practice, meaning that they provide a general service to a range of organisations, not just to one. ICSA: The Governance Institute's 'Directory of members' (more specifically, its register of 'members in public practice') is available on its website.[1]

One thing that you need to recognise is that the Chartered Secretary qualification is generally concerned with companies (although ICSA: The Governance Institute does now also provide a Certificate in Charity Law and Governance). In addition, most chartered secretaries in private practice work predominately for small commercial businesses. If you are seeking support from a chartered secretary, you should first ensure that they have experience with your type of legal form (e.g. company, charitable incorporated organisation or trust) and with organisations in the voluntary sector. Even if your organisation is a company, it is most

---

[1] 'Directory of members' [web page], ICSA: The Governance Institute, 2018, www.icsa.org.uk/directory-of-members?tabnum=2, accessed 15 May 2018.

likely to be a company limited by guarantee, whereas many chartered secretaries will be more familiar with companies limited by shares.

Solicitors

Some legal firms also provide secretarial services. This is an option to consider, particularly if your own firm of solicitors provides these services. If you are looking at using a legal firm, make sure that you find out the qualifications and experience of the staff who will provide the service. Are they lawyers (and, if so, does this have an impact on costs)? Are they legal executives? Are they chartered secretaries? If you are seeking support from one of these firms, you should also ensure (as outlined for chartered secretaries) that they have experience with your type of legal form and with organisations in the voluntary sector.

Accountants

Likewise, some accountancy firms also provide secretarial services. This is an option to consider, particularly if your own firm of accountants provides these services. As for chartered secretaries and solicitors, find out the qualifications and expertise of the staff who will provide the service and ask about their relevant experience with your type of legal form and the voluntary sector.

Choosing to outsource a board secretary

Before making the final decision to outsource a board secretary, there are three key points that you will need to consider:

- You will need to **think about what you need**. Outsourced secretaries usually deal with compliance matters, maintenance of registers and records, and providing specific advice when requested. It is more unusual for them to deal with the servicing of board and committee meetings, and it may be better for you to retain the minute-taking of meetings in-house.
- You will need to **specify exactly what services you want**. It is unlikely that an outsourced service will cover all of the aspects of the proposed role description. If it can, this will likely be at a high cost.
- You will need to **pay for an outsourced service**. While a number of commercial firms, such as lawyers, undertake pro bono work for charities and voluntary organisations, this is usually for specific pieces of work rather than an ongoing service such as acting as secretary.

Once you are satisfied that you wish to outsource the role of board secretary, there are some questions you should ask before committing to a specific service:

- If you are a charity, have you checked that the firm has worked with other charities and is familiar with charity law?
- If you are a company, have you checked that the firm is familiar with companies limited by guarantee and has the systems in place to support this structure? (Most company secretarial software is designed for companies limited by shares.)
- If you are not a company, have you checked that the firm understands your legal form and the law and compliance requirements that apply?
- Is the person who will be providing the services professionally qualified (such as a lawyer or holder of an ICSA: The Governance Institute qualification)?
- Does the person have knowledge of best practice in corporate governance for the sector?
- Does the person have experience of servicing board meetings and skills in taking minutes (if required)?

Choosing not to have a board secretary

Alternatively, as long as you are not a registered society, your organisation can choose not to have a board secretary. You must first check your constitution to ensure that it is not a requirement, or that it is removable if it is indeed a requirement.

Note that, if your organisation is a company, the board will have to specifically authorise a person or persons who can file documents with Companies House on its behalf. This authorisation should be taken down in the minutes too.

Different ways of working: who does what?

If you intend to have no board secretary, or if the role is being outsourced and your intention is that the outsourced board secretary will take on only key aspects of the role, it is a good idea to be very clear about who will take on which of the responsibilities of a secretary. It is essential to know who does what. There is often a lack of understanding of what needs to happen to ensure that an organisation is adequately governed and is operating in compliance with its regulatory requirements, so it is wise to set this out on paper. Table 4.1 is a model template that can be used. It assumes that the work will be split between three people, but you can adapt it as necessary if more or fewer people are required.

Table 4.1   Splitting out the role of board secretary

Elements of role	[Name]	[Name]	[Name]
Board meetings			
Organising board meetings			
Organising committee meetings			
Ensuring board committees are constituted in compliance with the terms of reference and that their membership is regularly reviewed and refreshed			
Drafting meeting agendas with the chair and/or the chief executive and advising on the content and organisation of papers for each meeting			
Collecting, organising and distributing such information, documents or other papers required for each meeting			
Ensuring that all minutes of board meetings are kept and that the minute books are maintained with certified copies of the minutes			
Ensuring that all minutes of committee meetings are kept and that the minute books are maintained with certified copies of the minutes			
General meetings (if applicable)			
Ensuring that an annual general meeting is held in accordance with legal requirements and the constitution			
Preparing and issuing notices of meetings and distributing proxy forms			
Ensuring that proxy forms are correctly processed and that the voting is carried out accurately			
Co-ordinating the administration of meetings and ensuring that appropriate minutes are kept			

Elements of role	[Name]	[Name]	[Name]
Constitution			
Ensuring that the organisation complies with its constitution, and drafting and incorporating amendments in accordance with correct procedures			
Registers (as applicable)			
Maintaining all statutory registers [*list each register*]			
Statutory returns (as applicable)			
Filing information with the Registrar of Companies, Charity Commission or Financial Conduct Authority to report certain changes regarding the organisation or to comply with requirements for periodic filing			
Report and accounts			
Co-ordinating the publication and distribution of the annual report and accounts in particular, and preparing the directors' report			
Corporate governance			
Continually reviewing developments in corporate governance			
Induction of board members			
Advising and assisting the board members on their duties and responsibilities			
Company identity			
Ensuring all of the legal requirements in regard to stationery and display of name are met, including in electronic communications and/or website(s)			
Establishing a summary of matters reserved for decision by the board, a scheme of delegation and so on			
Supporting board succession planning			
Helping to develop and support board performance evaluations and skills audits			

Outcomes and actions

After reading this chapter, you should have some ideas about other ways of working if your organisation does not want to have a board secretary. If you decide to keep the role but to outsource it, you should ensure that there is clarity about what you want to outsource and that you choose a provider with the necessary skills. If your organisation wants to do without a named secretary, there needs to be clarity about who will take on each of the core roles of a secretary.

5 What type is your organisation?

A fundamental thing that a secretary needs to understand is what legal form their organisation takes. This may seem like a simple question, but it is one that causes quite a lot of confusion. As board secretary, you have a key role in ensuring that your organisation works within the rules and regulations that govern it. You also need to ensure it operates within its constitution, so you will need to locate the constitution, read it and understand it. To be able to do all of this, it is essential that you understand the legal form of your organisation.

Within the voluntary sector, there are many different legal forms. Your organisation's type will usually be determined by its size, its age and the type of work that it does. It can also be influenced by whether or not it is a charity – although sometimes the question of charitable status can also be a matter of uncertainty (see chapter 6).

The principal types of legal form within the voluntary sector are:

- trust;
- unincorporated members' association;
- company limited by guarantee;
- community interest company (CIC);
- community benefit society;
- co-operative society;
- chartered body;
- charitable incorporated organisation (CIO).

Each will be described later in turn, and they are summarised in table 5.1 on page 45.

Incorporation

Some types of legal form mean that an organisation is incorporated and some mean that it is unincorporated. Incorporation means that an organisation is a 'corporate entity'. This means that it has a legal personality – the law recognises the organisation as a person. All in its own right, an incorporated organisation can enter into contracts, sue and be sued, and own assets and land. It exists separately from the people who run it. In contrast, an unincorporated organisation has no legal personality of its own – it is no more than the sum of its parts.

This means that if someone wants to sue a company (which is an example of an incorporated body) they sue the company itself. However, if they want to sue a trust, which is unincorporated, the trustees are sued as individuals because the trust does not exist as a legal entity in its own right – the law does not recognise it as a legal person.

The following are incorporated:

* company limited by guarantee;
* CIC;
* community benefit society;
* co-operative society;
* chartered body;
* CIO.

The following are unincorporated:

* trust;
* unincorporated members' association.

There are two main difficulties of being an unincorporated organisation. These concern liability, ownership of property and entering into contracts.

Liability

The board members of an unincorporated organisation (and sometimes its members) have unlimited personal liability. This applies even if they act in a completely reasonable way. They are responsible for all of the organisation's debts, they are the ones who enter into contracts (including employment contracts) and they are the ones who are sued. This liability can be even greater than you would expect as it does not necessarily need to be spread evenly between all the board members. The rules in these types of legal cases mean that the person who brings the case to court is entitled to sue all or any of the board members for the full amount of the loss. If there are ten board members and the amount to be sued for is £100,000, the person taking the action does not need to take it against all of the board members. They can pick one board member and sue them individually for the full amount. Board members can insure themselves against these liabilities, but the prospect of being sued in this way can still appear rather frightening to many prospective board members. Be aware that the level of protection an insurance policy offers will vary according to circumstances and will be subject to exclusions and limitations.

In an incorporated organisation, all members and board members are protected by limited liability. It is the organisation that is liable, not the individuals. A board member is only liable if they breach their legal duty as a board member.

In an unincorporated organisation, the board members are liable whether or not they have breached their duties. In an incorporated organisation, these liabilities only arise if duties have been breached. However, it is important to note that in an incorporated organisation the duties are owed to the organisation (or, in some instances, the shareholders or members) so it is for the organisation to take any action regarding a breach.

Whether or not the organisation is incorporated, action may also be taken in the following circumstances:

- action may be taken to disqualify a company director who has breached their duties;
- action may be taken to disqualify a charity trustee from acting as a trustee;
- the Charity Commission may take action to remove a charity trustee in a registered charity who has breached their duties (removal as a trustee will usually follow a statutory inquiry – where a trustee has breached their duties, the courts can also make them liable to repay any financial loss they have caused to the charity);
- the Charity Commission may take further action as a result of a statutory inquiry into a charity;
- under the Insolvency Act 1986, a company director may be personally liable for wrongful or fraudulent trading in the context of the insolvency of a company;
- the Health and Safety at Work Act 1974 places a duty on all employers to ensure (as far as possible) the health and safety at work of their employees. The Act says that, if an offence is committed by an incorporated organisation and there has been any neglect by the director, that director is also personally liable.[1] Breaches of the act may result in criminal sanctions.

Ownership of property and entering into contracts

In an unincorporated organisation, as the organisation cannot hold property, it needs to be held by individuals on the organisation's behalf. This will usually be the board members, but property can be held by separate people, sometimes called 'holding' or 'custodian' trustees. This

---

[1] 'Health and Safety at Work Act 1974' [web page], UK Government, 1974, www.legislation.gov.uk/ukpga/1974/37/section/37, Section 37, accessed 13 December 2017.

can, however, create some serious complexities. If the board members hold the property, every time the board composition changes, the title of the property will need to change. It can also be quite complex to enter into contracts and keep them up to date.

It is much simpler if the property and contracts can be held in the name of the organisation itself, as they can be in an incorporated organisation.

Types of organisation

Trust

A trust is formed when someone gives money or property to another person, entrusting it to them to be used for a specified purpose. It is one of the simplest types of organisation to create. As they are so simple, trusts can even be set up verbally, although it is more common for them to be established with a trust deed.

Although they are less commonly used today, trusts were traditionally one of the most commonly used forms for charities. You can see this in the fact that the terms 'trust' and 'trustee' are associated with charities and the fact that it is quite common for a charity to have 'trust' in its name, even if it is no longer set up in this way. This legal form also sits well with the more traditional notion of charity as philanthropy.

A trust does not have to be charitable; however, the most common type of non-charitable trust is a family trust (meaning it is set up to benefit children or grandchildren), so among voluntary sector organisations if an organisation is a trust it is most likely to be a charity.

A trust is unincorporated, so is a less suitable form if your organisation wants to own assets, employ staff or enter into contracts. As it is unincorporated, the trustees carry unlimited liability and so their personal assets are at risk. Also, while there are both charitable and non-charitable trusts, it is not an ideal legal form to use if you do not intend to be a charity.

Bear in mind that a charity can use the word trust in its title without officially being established in this legal form. For example, The National Trust is not a trust in its legal form; it was established by an Act of Parliament: the National Trust Act 1907.[2] Charitable companies can use the word trust, and many do so to indicate charitable status. Remember,

---

[2] *National Trust Act 1907–1971* [PDF], Parliamentary Scheme, 1907–1971, www.nationaltrust.org.uk/documents/download-national-trust-acts-1907-1971-post-order-2005.pdf, accessed 13 December 2017.

when seeking to identify an organisation's legal form, look behind its name.

Trusts: key things to look out for

- Your constitution will usually be called a trust deed (there are various forms of deed including wills, settlements and deeds of gift).
- Your board members will probably be called trustees.
- You will not have members (although you may use this term informally for supporters).
- You are most likely to be a grant-giving organisation.
- You will probably be a charity.
- You will be unincorporated.
- You will be more likely to be an older organisation.

Unincorporated members' association

An unincorporated members' association is another simple type of organisation. It is effectively created by a group of people coming together with a shared aim, without a profit motive. Like trusts, unincorporated members' associations can be created with no written agreement or documents, but they typically have a constitution or rules. There is no legal framework supporting unincorporated members' associations. They effectively work via the members' agreements between themselves and, in a more formal way, a constitution can act as a contract between the members.

Unincorporated members' associations share many of the disadvantages of trusts, as they are also unincorporated. The organisation cannot enter into contracts, sue or be sued, and its board members or trustees are those at risk if the organisation itself is sued. In certain situations, the members also carry unlimited liability.

Unincorporated members' associations are possibly one of the most common forms of voluntary organisation, especially if small, local groups are included. For example, it is very common for groups of friends of schools to be set up in this way. Other common examples include local community groups and sports clubs. Many organisations begin to operate in this way and then seek to incorporate at a later stage.

This legal form can seem very well suited to groups that want to represent a wide group of people, who can become members. However, its unincorporated status can cause difficulties.

Unincorporated members' associations: key things to look out for

- You will have members.
- You will probably work in quite an informal way through volunteers.
- Your work is likely to have a local, community or sports-related focus.
- You will be unincorporated.
- You may be quite a newly formed organisation.

Company limited by guarantee

The company is the legal form that you will come across most often in your daily life, but you will probably associate this form with commercial organisations rather than voluntary organisations. People are often surprised that a not-for-profit or charitable organisation can be a company, but it is one of the most common ways for a voluntary organisation to be established. Although it may seem like a less suitable form, it can easily be adapted to not-for-profit and charitable contexts. Although it carries additional regulatory oversight by Companies House, this is fairly minimal. It can be very quick and easy to set up a company, and it can provide useful mechanisms, as long as you accept the ongoing legal and regulatory obligations.

The key reason to be a company is that companies are incorporated, and becoming a company is the easiest way to achieve incorporation. All companies have owners (shareholders or, especially in a voluntary organisation, members), and when a company is set up its incorporation creates a separation between the 'owners' of the company and the company itself. This is called the 'veil of incorporation'. Additionally, the owners (the shareholders or members) are not the people who run the company – this is done by the board. It is possible to have the same people undertaking both roles – being a shareholder or a member and being a board member (company director) – but these are still two distinct roles.

As an incorporated body, a company has a distinct legal personality. It is distinct from those who set it up. If the company fails, the people who set it up, or who own it, can walk away from it. In most instances, they have no liabilities (there are some rare exceptions). In addition, board members are distinct from the company and so they also have limited liability. This is clearly very advantageous to companies and the people who set them up. For this reason, as a balance to this benefit, companies have certain requirements regarding transparency and reporting. A company has to prepare accounts and it has to make them available to its members. A company has to be open about who its board members are, and it has to file this information and other information at Companies House.

There are two main types of company: a company limited by shares and a company limited by guarantee. Companies limited by guarantee are the form that is most common within the voluntary sector, and it is usually not possible to register a charitable company limited by shares with the Charity Commission.

In a company limited by shares, the shareholders are the members of the company. They each purchase shares in it and that determines the proportion of the company that they own.

In a company limited by guarantee, instead of purchasing shares, the members guarantee that if the company is wound up and has debts which need to be honoured, they will pay a certain amount towards those debts. This may seem like a frightening responsibility, but the reality is that the amount of the guarantee is usually very low, often £1. A member's liability is limited to the amount of their guarantee.

Companies limited by shares are the more common form in the commercial sector, as they are designed around investment. A shareholder puts their investment into a company by purchasing shares. They hope that the company will make a profit, so that they can take dividends on that profit. They also hope that the value of the company will grow, so their share of the company will be worth more. Companies limited by guarantee do not pay dividends, and the value of the guarantee does not vary or increase. Therefore, this type of company is more suitable for groups of people who come together to achieve a particular aim rather than seeking to profit themselves.

A company must have at least one member (a shareholder or guarantor). It must also have at least one director (within the voluntary sector, usually more than one). Being a member and being a director are two separate roles. While it is quite common for directors to also act as members, meaning the same people may carry out both roles, do not forget that they are always separate and distinct.

When people see the word 'Limited' or 'Ltd' at the end of an organisation's name, it usually indicates to them that they are dealing with a company. However, it is important to note that community benefit and co-operative societies also use the word Limited in their name. Also, even more importantly, a company can apply to leave Limited out of its name if it is a charity or sports club, or if it is limited by guarantee and meets certain requirements regarding its purposes, and the non-distribution of its assets. This means that many not-for-profit companies do not use Limited in their name. Therefore, you should not assume that just because your organisation does not have the word Limited in its name it is not a company. Charities such as Scope and the Guide Dogs for the Blind Association are charitable companies.

Companies are governed by the Companies Act 2006. They are subject to regulatory oversight by Companies House and are required to submit annual accounts and to file certain information at Companies House. They also have legal requirements regarding the records and registers that they keep. This is covered in more detail later in this chapter.

Companies limited by guarantee: key things to look out for

*   You will have members, but these may be the same people as your board members.
*   Your board members may be called directors.
*   Your constitution will be called articles (or memorandum and articles).
*   You will be incorporated.
*   You may have Limited or Ltd in your name, but remember that many types of not-for-profit companies will have applied not to use Limited or Ltd.
*   You will have a company registration number.

Community interest company

A fairly new type of company is the community interest company (CIC), which has been in existence since 2005. These were created to be used by social enterprises that are not charitable. It is not possible to have a charitable CIC – it is a legal form for businesses that trade with social purposes. They are similar to charities in some ways, particularly as their assets are locked and cannot be distributed to members or shareholders. However, they do allow some distribution of profits. A CIC is a company and so it can be set up as a company limited by guarantee or a company limited by shares. If the CIC is limited by shares, it can pay dividends to shareholders (within prescribed limits). This legal form is also suitable for somebody who wants to set up an organisation for a social purpose but then draw a salary from it.

A CIC has to be able to show that it is established for the community interest, meaning that a reasonable person would consider that the company's activities were for the benefit of the community. This is a much broader test than that for charities, but it does need to be considered.

A key feature of a CIC is the asset lock. The articles of a CIC are drafted so that assets (other than permissible dividends) cannot be distributed to members or shareholders. Also, if the assets are transferred to another body, they must be transferred at the full value (unless it is for the benefit of the community) to an organisation specified in the articles or approved by the CIC Regulator. Many not-for-profit companies (not charities) have similar clauses in their constitution, but – crucially – they can change them if they wish through a vote. In contrast, like a charity, where prior consent of the Charity Commission would be needed to a relevant alteration, a CIC is prevented from removing such a clause from its articles, unless it obtains prior regulatory consent from the CIC Regulator.

This means CICs have some similar restrictions to those placed on charities but do not benefit from the tax exemptions that are available to charities. CICs, along with other types of social enterprise, may benefit from community interest tax relief but they are still liable to pay corporation tax.

In addition to having to make the usual returns and filings at Companies House, CICs are regulated by the CIC Regulator. A CIC's articles need to take a particular form and there are statutory clauses that cannot be changed without the prior consent of the CIC Regulator. Furthermore, a CIC must submit a CIC report to the regulator every year, at the same time as its accounts. A CIC must also pay additional fees to the regulator, as well as Companies House fees.

Community interest companies: key things to look out for

- You will have members, but these may be the same people as your board members.
- Your board members may be called directors.
- Your constitution will be called articles (or memorandum and articles).
- You will be incorporated.
- You will have CIC or Community Interest Company at the end of your name.
- You will have been formed after 2005.
- You cannot be a charity.

Community benefit societies and co-operative societies

Both community benefit societies and co-operative societies fall under the heading of what used to be called industrial and provident societies (IPS) and are now called registered societies. A community benefit society is a society set up to benefit the community as a whole. A co-operative society is one set up to benefit its own members. Because of this, a co-operative society is usually not charitable. If a registered society is a charity, it will usually be a community benefit society. This is a legal form that is most commonly used by registered providers of social housing. The form is not widely used by other types of organisation, as registered societies are quite complex to set up and not commonly understood.

Community benefit societies and co-operative societies are incorporated bodies, just like companies, and so their board members and members have limited liability. Like companies, they must have at least one member and at least one director (board member), which are separate and distinct roles. Again, the two roles can be carried out by the same people. Community benefit societies and co-operative societies are registered with the Financial Conduct Authority (FCA) rather than Companies House. If the community benefit society is also a registered provider of social housing, it will also be regulated by the Regulator of Social Housing (previously the Homes and Community Agency).

Community benefit societies and co-operative societies are governed by a number of pieces of legislation. The Co-operative and Community Benefit Societies Act 2014 replaced the IPS legal form with two new legal forms (community benefit society and co-operative society) and consolidated previous IPS legislation.

Before the act came into force, all societies registered in this way were legally referred to as IPSs. Now, pre-existing societies are referred to as registered societies and any new societies are referred to as co-operative societies or community benefit societies.

Community benefit societies and co-operative societies: key things to look out for

- You will have shareholders, but these may be the same people as your board members.
- Your constitution will be called rules.
- You will be incorporated.
- You will have Limited or Ltd at the end of your name.

Chartered body

Chartered status is a very old way of conferring corporate status, and incorporation, on an organisation. It pre-dates the more modern form of registered companies, which are governed by the Companies Act 2006. At one time it was the only way of gaining incorporation, but it has now been overtaken by the registration of companies. Chartered status is conferred on an organisation by the Privy Council. It is less common for chartered status to be granted now, and the right to become a chartered body is generally restricted to professional bodies and (in rarer cases) some charities. There are quite strict criteria for becoming a chartered body. A professional body needs to show that it is of sufficient size, that it is financially sound and that it represents a unique field of activity. It also needs to demonstrate how the regulation of its profession would be to the benefit of the public. Chartered bodies are generally professional bodies but there are also some chartered charities, such as the Royal National Lifeboat Institution as well as some academic/learned societies and universities. A chartered body may be charitable, but it need not be. Both the Chartered Institute of Marketing and the Chartered Institute of Internal Auditors are chartered but not charitable. The Chartered Institution of Building Services Engineers, however, is an example of a chartered professional body that is a charity.

Chartered bodies: key things to look out for

- You are likely to be a professional body.
- Your constitution is called charter.
- You will be incorporated.

Charitable incorporated organisation

The charitable incorporated organisation (CIO) is a newer type of legal form, specifically designed for charities. It can only be used by charities, so if your organisation is a CIO it must be a charity. CIOs were created by the Charities Act 2006 but did not come into existence until some time after that. In Scotland, the first SCIOs (Scottish Charitable Incorporated Organisations) were established in 2011 but the first CIOs in England and Wales were not registered until 2013. The CIO is becoming quite a popular legal form, with the case now being that more than half of new charity registrations are for CIOs. From April 2016 to March 2017, there were 6,045 charities registered by the Charity Commission, 3,684 of which were CIOs.[3]

The purpose of the CIO is to give charities an incorporated legal form without the need for dual regulation and registration. If you look at table 5.1, you will see that for all the incorporated legal forms other than a CIO, there is another regulator as well as the Charity Commission. For CIOs, the Charity Commission is the sole regulator.

A CIO is incorporated like a company, so the trustees have limited liability. As an incorporated body it can hold assets, employ staff, enter into contracts, sue

---

[3] *Charity Commission Annual Report and Accounts 2016–17* [PDF], Charity Commission, 2017, www.gov.uk/government/uploads/system/uploads/attachment_data/file/628747/Charity_Commission_Annual_Report_and_Accounts_2016_17_web.pdf, accessed 8 April 2018.

and be sued. Like a company, it has to have members as well as a board (the trustees), although it can have just one member. The Charity Commission distinguishes between two types of CIO (and issues two different model constitutions, one for each type): the association CIO (which has a body of members who are distinct from the trustees) and the foundation CIO (where the members and the trustees are one and the same people).

Being a CIO can seem like a simpler way of being incorporated without having to become a company. However, there are a number of CIO-specific legal rules and requirements and some of the small charity filing exemptions do not apply to CIOs. In addition, it should be remembered that there are a number of advantages in being a charitable company. It is fairly simple and quick to set up a charitable company; what takes more time is registration with the Charity Commission. In addition, it is arguable that the company is a more widely recognised legal form, which can present a number of advantages in contracting and working with third parties. This also means that there is an established body of law behind the legal form.

One of the real advantages of CIOs as a form is for smaller charities. At the present time, charity registration is not an option for charities with an income of under £5,000 each year unless they are registered as CIOs. The Charity Commission just does not have the resources to offer registration to smaller charities. In contrast, if a small charity wants to be registered with the Charity Commission, becoming a CIO is a means of becoming registered without having to meet this income requirement.

Although registration with the Charity Commission carries obligations for all CIOs (regardless of size or type and scale of activities) regarding annual returns and filing of accounts, these are not onerous and there are a number of real advantages to being a registered charity. Registration clearly shows that an organisation is a charity and gives security to funders and donors. Charities with a registration number can find that it helps them to fundraise. Having said this, while the requirements are not onerous, they do require a greater degree of organisation and compliance than is needed for a small unincorporated organisation.

Charitable incorporated organisations: key things to look out for

- You will have members, but these may be the same people as your board members.
- Your constitution will be called a constitution.
- You will be incorporated.
- You will be a charity.
- You will have been formed since 2013 (in England and Wales), or, if you are an SCIO, you will have been registered since 2011.

Table 5.1 Legal forms

	Incorporated	Charitable or non-charitable	Members as well as board members	Regulator(s)	Limited liability
Trust	No	Charitable or non-charitable	No	Charity Commission (if applicable)	No
Unincorporated members' association	No	Charitable or non-charitable	Yes	Charity Commission (if applicable)	No
Company limited by guarantee	Yes	Charitable or non-charitable	Yes	Charity Commission (if applicable); Companies House	Yes
Community interest company	Yes	Non-charitable	Yes	Companies House (and CIC Regulator)	Yes
Community benefit society	Yes	Charitable or non-charitable	Yes	Financial Conduct Authority; Regulator of Social Housing (for registered providers of social housing)	Yes
Co-operative society	Yes	Usually non-charitable	Yes	Financial Conduct Authority; Regulator of Social Housing (for registered providers of social housing)	Yes
Chartered body	Yes	Charitable or non-charitable	Yes or no	Charity Commission (if applicable); Privy Council	Yes
Charitable incorporated organisation	Yes	Charitable	Yes or no	Charity Commission (if applicable)	Yes

Ways to identify your legal form

You may need to look in various places to confirm the legal form of your organisation:

- Check your constitution – its title may give you an indication of your organisation's legal form (see chapter 7). It is also quite common for the constitution to describe an organisation's legal form.
- If your organisation is a registered company, it will be on the register held at Companies House, which is also available online at http://wck2.companieshouse.gov.uk. This will apply if your organisation is a company limited by guarantee or a CIC. The Companies House register extends beyond companies, now including details of other incorporated bodies – CIOs, registered societies and chartered bodies. For all of these types of bodies, the listing does not include details of the organisation but it does describe their legal form and so is a useful way of establishing whether your organisation is incorporated. For CIOs, as well as the basic details shown on the Companies House website, there is a link to their entry on the Charity Commission's website.
- If your organisation is a community benefit society or a co-operative society, it will be on the register held by the mutuals team at the FCA and available online at https://mutuals.fsa.gov.uk.
- Check the name of your organisation – this may give you an indication. But remember that not all organisations that use the word Trust are indeed trusts. At the same time, many not-for-profit companies are exempt from using Limited or Ltd, and community benefit societies and co-operative societies also use Limited or Ltd.
- Consider whether your organisation is a charity or not (see chapter 6) as this could limit the legal forms available to it.

Changing legal form

Sometimes an organisation decides that it needs to change legal form. The most common scenario is when an unincorporated organisation decides that it wishes to incorporate. It is very common for organisations to grow and develop from fairly informal working arrangements. As the organisation begins to develop, it may adopt a constitution and become an unincorporated members' association. Over time it may take ownership of land, begin to employ people or enter into contracts. As the risks grow and the potential liability of board members becomes more of an issue, the organisation may look at incorporation.

While you can change legal form, this can usually only happen by creating a new organisation in the form that you want it to be, then transferring all of the assets of your organisation to the new organisation. There are some rare exceptions – for example, a company limited by guarantee can change into a CIC. (As a CIC is also a type of company, in this scenario the organisation does not change legal form as such and so does not need to create a new organisation.) This means that changing legal form is often more complex than you might think. If your organisation is a registered charity, the new organisation will need to be registered with the Charity Commission, meaning you will have a new registration number.

So, although you can change forms, it is not a good idea to plan for this in the life of your organisation. If your organisation is just beginning to form but you are planning to be incorporated one day, it is worthwhile incorporating right from the start rather than changing the legal form later on in your organisation's life.

Duties of company directors

If your organisation is a company, your board members are the company directors and their duties are set out in the Companies Act 2006. These duties are as follows:

A duty to act within powers

A director must always act within the constitution of the company and can only use their powers as a director for the purposes for which they were given.

A duty to promote the success of the company

This is an interesting duty as it relates to one of the few sections of the Companies Act where there is a difference specified between commercial and non-commercial companies. Promoting the success of the company is defined as acting for the benefit of members, but Section 172 of the Companies Act goes on to say that if the company has purposes, or objects, that are different from or broader than the benefit of the members, promoting the success of the company needs to be interpreted as acting to achieve those purposes.[4] Most voluntary organisations that are companies have purposes, or objects, and this means that their board members have a duty to act in furtherance of those purposes, and not in the interest of

[4] 'Companies Act 2006' [web page], UK Government, 2006, www.legislation.gov.uk/ukpga/2006/46/section/172, Section 172(2), accessed 13 December 2017.

the members. This applies even if the organisation is a membership organisation.

The Companies Act states that, when exercising this duty, the company directors should have regard to:

(a) the likely consequences of any decision in the long term,

(b) the interests of the company's employees,

(c) the need to foster the company's business relationships with suppliers, customers and others,

(d) the impact of the company's operations on the community and the environment,

(e) the desirability of the company maintaining a reputation for high standards of business conduct, and

(f) the need to act fairly as between members of the company.[5]

A duty to exercise independent judgement

Company directors should seek and consider professional advice, and they can act in accordance with it – but they must always use their own judgement in regard to whether or not to follow the advice they receive. This duty also means that directors must act independently; they cannot act on behalf of another or as a representative, even if they are appointed by another body.

A duty to exercise reasonable care, skill and diligence

There are two aspects to this duty. Firstly, there is an obligation to reach a reasonable standard of care, skill and diligence, which applies to all directors. However, this duty also means that if a director has particular knowledge, skill or experience they are expected to bring that to the role and apply it. For example, a director who is a qualified accountant is expected to apply their knowledge of accountancy. It is not acceptable for them to say that an ordinary person would not have had that knowledge and so it did not need to be used.

A duty to avoid conflicts of interest

This means that, as well as declaring any conflicts of interest, a director has a duty to withdraw from any decision-making where there is or may be a conflict of interest.

---

[5] 'Companies Act 2006' [web page], UK Government, 2006, www.legislation.gov.uk/ukpga/2006/46/section/172, Section 172(1), accessed 13 December 2017.

It is possible for a company to consent to a conflict of interest, enabling the director to take part in considering a matter (though in such cases the conflict still needs to be declared). This consent can be given by the members of the company (it can be given retrospectively) or by the other directors of the company. However, it must be remembered that if your organisation is a charitable company, there are also requirements under the common law of charities for conflicts to be avoided. These requirements apply even if a company has consented to a conflict. In this way, a charitable company needs to be aware that the ability to permit conflicts of interest is more limited than in a non-charitable company.

A duty to reject benefits from third parties

A company may authorise such benefits, either via its shareholders or via the board itself, and this can enable board members to accept gifts and hospitality. However, without this authorisation, the default duty is to not accept such benefits. Note that, in a charitable company, such an authorisation cannot be given because of the charity law rules which prevent charity trustees from receiving personal and private benefits.

A duty to declare any interest in proposed transactions or arrangements

Note that this duty is in regard to 'proposed transactions or arrangements' – hence, the duty is to make the declaration before the transaction is carried out.[6] Also, even if a company has authorised a conflict of interest, it still needs to be declared.

In addition, there is a legal obligation to declare interests in existing transactions and arrangements. For example, a new trustee must provide details of their pre-existing interests.

Outcomes and actions

After reading this chapter, you should understand the various legal forms that voluntary organisations can take, along with the advantages and disadvantages of each legal form. When reading this book, you must keep in mind an understanding of the legal form that your own organisation takes. You should take some time now to work this out (see page 46 for ways that you can do this). This chapter also provides information on changing legal form, which is an option that you may want to consider.

---

[6] 'Companies Act 2006' [web page], UK Government, 2006, www.legislation.gov.uk/ukpga/2006/46/section/177, Section 177, accessed 6 June 2018.

6 Is your organisation a charity?

A key issue that will affect your work as a board secretary is whether or not your organisation is a charity. The voluntary sector is made up of not-for-profit organisations and charities. Not-for-profit organisations do not have a profit motive and are often focused on meeting community needs or providing a public benefit, but they are not charities and so do not need to consider the legal restrictions and regulations that being a charity brings. If your organisation is a charity, it is bound by charity law and you will need to consider this. If it is a registered charity, you will also need to consider the regulatory requirements of the Charity Commission.

The question of whether your organisation is a charity is different from the question of what type of legal structure your organisation has. In fact, charities can take on a number of different legal structures. While some types of legal structure are only available for charities (such as community interest companies) and others are not suitable for charities (such as share companies), many types of legal structure are used by both charities and non-charities.

A common misunderstanding about charities is that registration with the Charity Commission makes an organisation a charity. Registration with the Charity Commission is required if your charity's income is over £5,000 a year (unless it is exempt or excepted from registration with the Charity Commission – the rules on this are set out later in this chapter) or if it is a charitable incorporated organisation (CIO). A large number of charities are not registered with the Charity Commission because their income is too small. If this does not apply to your charity, it is a legal requirement for the trustees to register the charity with the Charity Commission.

It is probably this misunderstanding that is at the heart of misconceptions about the number of charities in England and Wales. On 31 March 2017 there were approximately 167,000 registered charities in England and Wales and there were approximately 6,000 new registrations from April 2016 to March 2017.[1] However, in 2012 the National Audit Office estimated

---

[1] *Charity Commission Annual Report and Accounts 2016–17* [PDF], Charity Commission, 2017, www.gov.uk/government/uploads/system/uploads/attachment_

that there were perhaps another 180,000 charities that were excepted from registration (due to their size or other reasons).[2] There were also about 11,000 exempt charities (which are also not required to register with the Charity Commission). Putting all of this together, there are potentially 358,000 charities in England and Wales, perhaps more. It is also the case that there are many charities out there that do not necessarily recognise themselves as charities. If your organisation meets the criteria set out below, it is a charity – even if you were not aware of that fact.

The Charities Act 2011 states that a charity is an organisation which is:

* established for charitable purposes only;
* for the public benefit;
* subject to the control of the High Court's charity law jurisdiction.[3]

You need to be aware that not everything that benefits the community or is a good cause is charitable. There are restrictions on this broad definition.

* A charity cannot have political purposes.
* A charity cannot have purposes that are illegal under the law of England and Wales.
* An organisation registered as a charity in England and Wales has to be subject to jurisdiction in England and Wales and not the jurisdiction of any other country or area (including Scotland, Northern Ireland, the Isle of Man and the Channel Islands).
* A charity must be independent of outside control – its trustees must always act in the interests of the charity and not on behalf of another party, even if that party appointed them.
* A charity must use all of its assets, surplus and profit in pursuit of its purpose. The clause in a charity's constitution that sets out this requirement is often called a non-distribution clause. There will often be exceptions drafted into the clause, such as allowing trustees to be beneficiaries or allowing trustees to enter into contracts with the charity if particular requirements are met. However, without such

---

data/file/628747/Charity_Commission_Annual_Report_and_Accounts_2016_17_web. pdf, accessed 13 December 2017.

[2] *Regulating Charities: A landscape review* [PDF], National Audit Office, 2012, www. nao.org.uk/wp-content/uploads/2012/07/Regulating_charities.pdf, p. 15, accessed 13 December 2017.

[3] 'The Charities Act 2011' [web page], UK Government, 2011, www.legislation.gov. uk/ukpga/2011/25/section/1, Section 1(1), accessed 13 December 2017; 'The Charities Act 2011' [web page], UK Government, 2011, www.legislation.gov.uk/ukpga/2011/25/ section/2, Section 2(1)(a), accessed 13 December 2017.

exceptions included within the clause or granted by the Charity Commission, the general rule of a charity is that trustees cannot receive any tangible benefit from the charity.

Charitable purposes are defined by the Charities Act 2011. They are sometimes also called the 'heads of charity'. The charitable purposes are:

(a) the prevention or relief of poverty;

(b) the advancement of education;

(c) the advancement of religion;

(d) the advancement of health or the saving of lives;

(e) the advancement of citizenship or community development;

(f) the advancement of the arts, culture, heritage or science;

(g) the advancement of amateur sport;

(h) the advancement of human rights, conflict resolution or reconciliation or the promotion of religious or racial harmony or equality and diversity;

(i) the advancement of environmental protection or improvement;

(j) the relief of those in need, by reason of youth, age, ill-health, disability, financial hardship or other disadvantage;

(k) the advancement of animal welfare;

(l) the promotion of the efficiency of the armed forces of the Crown, or of the efficiency of the police, fire and rescue services or ambulance services';

(m) and other purposes... recognised as charitable purposes.[4]

The list above is a general explanation of charitable purposes. There is greater complexity in regard to the definitions (such as the definition of religion), more information can be obtained from the Charity Commission (www.gov.uk/government/publications/charitable-purposes/charitable-purposes).

For your organisation to be a charity, its purposes need to fall under one or more of these purposes. You also need to show that the organisation is established for public benefit, which means showing that:

• the purpose is beneficial;

• any detriment or harm that results from the purpose does not outweigh the benefit;

• the benefit is to the public in general or to a sufficient section of the public;

• the purpose does not give rise to more than incidental personal benefit (e.g. for a trustee).

---

[4] 'Charities Act 2011' [web page], UK Government, 2011, www.legislation.gov.uk/ukpga/2011/25/section/3, Section 3, accessed 13 December 2017.

Example: charitable and non-charitable purposes

If you wanted to set up an organisation to provide housing and you wanted it to be charitable, you could have purposes that read:

> To provide housing and assistance to relieve poverty and to help those in need by reason of youth, age, ill-health, disability, financial hardship or other disadvantage.

However, you could not have purposes that read:

> To provide housing across the South East and to help those in need by reason of youth, age, ill-health, disability, financial hardship or other disadvantage.

This is because the provision of housing is not in itself a charitable purpose. It can only be a means of meeting a charitable purpose.

How to identify whether your organisation is a charity

The first question is: are you registered with the Charity Commission? If not, you will need to look for some of the following key features of a charity:

- Look at your organisation's purposes (sometimes called objects). You will find your purposes in your constitution, usually at the start. Is your organisation established for charitable purposes only? Your purposes do not have to be written in the same way as the charitable purposes as listed in the 2011 Charities Act, but they need to fall within one or more of those purposes. For example, if your purposes say 'to establish and manage a school', your organisation will fall under the head of 'the advancement of education' even though your constitution does not directly say that.

- Does your constitution have a non-distribution clause stating that any profits or surplus cannot usually be paid to the trustees or members – i.e. that they can only be used for the charity's purposes?

- Does your organisation meet the requirements concerning public benefit mentioned at the start of this chapter?

These are the main ways of identifying whether your organisation is a charity. Some other factors are less certain but worth considering:

- Are the members of your board called trustees? Note that this term is often used in non-charities to refer to the people who oversee the running of the organisation. However, in a charity, the board members are legally trustees, even if they are not called this.

- Does your constitution refer to your organisation as a charity or make other relevant references? An example of this could be a clause saying that on the winding up of the organisation any remaining assets can only be distributed to a charity with similar purposes.

Charity law and restrictions

Charities need to operate within charity law, and this comes from both common law (meaning court cases that set precedents) and from statutes. The common-law principles relevant to charities have broadly developed from trust law, but for modern-day charities most of the legal regulation comes from statutes. The key statutes that charities need to consider and comply with are:

- **The Trustee Act 2000:** The Trustee Act is of relevance for unincorporated charities. It was essentially drafted to give the trustees of these types of charity some powers that they were lacking regarding managing investments and trusts. Trustees of charitable companies and CIOs do not need to rely on these powers, and in fact the powers do not automatically apply to them in the same way as they do to unincorporated charities.
- **The Charities Act 2011:** This Act is a consolidating piece of legislation that replaced a number of statutes, including the Charities Act 1992 and the Charities Act 2006. It sets out most of the key provisions of charity law.
- **The Charities (Protection and Social Investment) Act 2016:** This Act strengthened the powers of the Charity Commission and made some other legal changes.

An interesting thing about charity law is that one key piece of it – the general legal duties of charity trustees – is still only set out in common law and not in statutory law. This is in contrast to the legal duties of company directors, which are included in the Companies Act 2006. The duties of charity trustees are considered later in this chapter (see page 59) and the duties of company directors are considered in chapter 5 (see page 47).

Being a charity has a number of benefits – principally the tax advantage that it provides. However, charity law also places restrictions on charities, and it is important that you understand these if your organisation is a charity. The key benefits of being a charity are:

- Being recognised as a charity can increase public confidence and trust, which is very helpful in fundraising. This is particularly the case for registered charities.

- Some types of grants and funding are only available to charities.
- Charities are exempt from paying corporation tax on any profits that they gain from primary-purpose trading (i.e. trading that is directly related to the charity's purposes and where the profits are used for the charity's charitable purposes) and from a small amount of commercial trading.
- Charities are eligible for relief from business rates – they are granted a mandatory 80% relief from non-domestic rates where the property is wholly or mainly used for charitable purposes. A local authority can also give discretionary relief of up to the full amount – i.e. the remaining 20%.
- Charities are eligible for Gift Aid relief on qualifying donations from individuals.
- Charities are eligible for stamp duty land tax relief on freehold property and leases acquired for charitable purposes.
- Charities do not have to pay VAT on some goods and services.
- For many charities, the fact that their status places a lock on their assets is an assurance to donors and funders. While many other types of voluntary organisation can have similar non-distribution clauses in their constitutions, there is the risk that these can be overturned by members and therefore a risk of the organisation's assets being redistributed.

The main restrictions that need to be considered are:
- There are restrictions on trading activities. As mentioned above, charities can engage in primary-purpose trading and can benefit from relief from corporation tax on the profits from this trading. However, once they begin to engage in other forms of trading, including trading to fundraise, that tax exemption ceases (beyond a small threshold) and the charity's trustees may be placing themselves at risk by misusing the charity's assets. This is why trading activities are often conducted via a trading subsidiary.
- There are restrictions on political activities. These restrictions are often envisaged as being wider than they are. While a charity cannot be established for a political purpose, it is still able to undertake campaigning and political activities provided these are in furtherance of the charitable purposes and are not prohibited by the constitution. However, a charity is meant to remain politically neutral and should never engage in any form of party political activity.
- Registered charities must comply with regulatory requirements, including the submission of annual returns and requirements relating to the preparation of annual accounts and returns. This means that

they need to make information about their finances, governance and activities publicly available. There are also things that the Charity Commission must be kept informed about, such as the reporting of serious incidents and updates on trustees.

- There is a presumption that trustees (board members) are unpaid. While there are a number of examples of board members being paid, there always needs to be explicit authority to do this – either from a clause in the constitution or from the Charity Commission.
- There is also a restriction on board members being beneficiaries of the charity or being paid for any services that they provide to the charity. Again, there needs to be explicit authority to do this – either from a clause in the constitution or from the Charity Commission giving authority. This means that a charity often cannot benefit anyone connected to the charity – for example, by employing a board member's family member or company – unless it had been authorised to do so.

Exempt and excepted charities

Definitions

Exempt charities are exempt from registration with and regulation by the Charity Commission.

Excepted charities are excepted from registration with the Charity Commission but can be regulated by the Charity Commission.

As previously mentioned, not all charities are registered with the Charity Commission – some because they are too small, but many because they fall into the categories of exempt or excepted charities. These are groupings that developed over time; they are types of charities where it was considered inappropriate or unnecessary for them to be registered with and regulated by the Charity Commission. These types of charity are still subject to charity law, but they are not required to register with the Charity Commission.

Historically, the primary reason why exempt charities were made exempt from direct regulation by the Charity Commission was because they were supervised by, or accountable to, another body. However, the Charities Act 2006 recognised that this had not always proved effective and that not all of these charities had been effectively regulated. The act therefore attempted to improve the way exempt charities were regulated. It stated that previously exempt charities must either have a principal regulator to regulate them as charities or come within the remit of Charity Commission regulation.

This promised to be quite a big change but in fact the extension of Charity Commission regulation to many of these charities has been staggered and it is still not fully in force.

Principal regulators were appointed by the government, with the intention being that they would usually be the charities' main regulator. A principal regulator will usually regulate charities for other purposes as well – for example, the Secretary of State for Education is the principal regulator of academy schools. The role of principal regulators is also to promote and monitor charities' compliance with charity law. They also work with the Charity Commission to help ensure that exempt charities are accountable to the public. While principal regulators cannot investigate charities themselves for failure to comply with charity law, they have the right to ask the Charity Commission to open an inquiry, if necessary.

Principal regulators were appointed for a number of types of exempt charity, but it was also agreed that some types of charity would no longer be exempt because there was no suitable body to act as their principal regulator. These included universities and other higher education institutions in Wales, student unions, the Church Commissioners, and the Representative Body of the Church in Wales. The Charity Commission could not take on all of the previously exempt charities so it was initially agreed that charities that had ceased to be exempt would only register with the Charity Commission if their income exceeded £100,000 per year, and this is still the case.

In addition, there are some exempt charities where it was initially expected that there would be principal regulators but principal regulators have not yet been appointed. An example is charitable community benefit societies that are registered providers of social housing. As of mid-2018, there does not appear to be any prospect of principal regulators being appointed for these organisations.

Exempt charities are not registered with the Charity Commission. This means that they do not have a registered charity number. The organisation's charitable status will have been recognised by HMRC for taxation purposes, and it is this acknowledgement which it will normally use to prove its charitable status. Exempt charities can apply to the Charity Commission for voluntary registration. However, the Charity Commission will only consider such applications in exceptional circumstances.

Exempt charities also do not have to comply with many of the Charities Act's requirements with regard to annual reports and accounts, although they still have a requirement to prepare accounts and to make them available. Their accounts are often in a different format from registered charity accounts, usually being designed to meet their principal regulator's requirements.

Exempt charities are not just exempt from registration with the Charity Commission; they are also exempt from its regulation. The Charity Commission can provide information and advice, and it can also make schemes and orders (a scheme is a legal document that changes, replaces or extends the purposes of a charity or otherwise deals with its administration). However, where there is a principal regulator, the Charity Commission can only use these powers after consultation with that regulator.

As well as exempt charities, there are excepted charities. These do not need to register with or submit annual returns to the Charity Commission. However, in all other ways, the Charity Commission regulates excepted charities just as it does registered charities. It can also use any and all of its powers in relation to excepted charities.

The following groups are excepted:
- churches and chapels belonging to some Christian denominations;
- charities that provide premises for some types of school;
- Scout and Guide groups;
- charitable service funds of the armed forces.

Just like exempt charities with no principal regulator, these types of charity will cease to be excepted and will need to register with the Charity Commission if their income exceeds £100,000.

Duties of charity trustees

If your organisation is a charity, your board members will be charity trustees and will have duties under charity law. These duties are established by common law and are not listed in any statute. While the two sets of duties are worded differently, in many ways there is real crossover between the duties of a company director (see chapter 5, page 47) and the duties of a charity trustee. This means that if your organisation is a charitable company and your board members are fulfilling the duties of charity trustees, they will also be meeting their duties as company directors. Therefore, in this situation, there is no need for board members to continually check whether they are complying with both sets of duties.

The duties of charity trustees are outlined on the following page.

A duty to act in accordance with law and the constitution

This means that your board members must have an understanding of the law that applies to the organisation, including an overview of the requirements of charity law. Board members also need to have a basic knowledge of the constitution, particularly the purposes of the charity. They must make sure that cases of 'object drift' never arise, meaning that they must make sure that the charity is carrying out the purposes for which it was set up and no other purposes.

A duty to act in the interests of the charity only

This duty means that a trustee can only act in the interests of the charity and cannot act on behalf of anyone else. Therefore, they cannot act as a representative. Even if they are appointed by another body, they cannot represent it.

This duty also means that trustees must avoid conflicts of interest by declaring them and then removing themselves from the discussion and from any decision-making. The Charity Commission takes a wide view of conflict, deeming it to include what it calls 'conflicts of loyalty'. A conflict of loyalty arises when a trustee's loyalty or duty to another person or organisation could prevent them from acting in the best interests of the charity.[5] Trustees also must not receive any benefit from the charity unless it is properly authorised and is clearly in the interests of the charity.

A duty to manage the affairs of the charity responsibly

Trustees have a responsibility to exercise sound judgement. They need to consider risks and not take undue risks. They need to take particular care when investing or borrowing. There are also some restrictions in charity law on selling land and property.

A duty to use reasonable skill and care in working as a trustee, applying what knowledge and experience they have

The law imposes a duty of care on the trustees of charities. As is the case in a company, the duty is greater if a trustee has any particular

---

[5] 'Conflicts of interest: A guide for charity trustees' [web page], Charity Commission, 2014, www.gov.uk/government/publications/conflicts-of-interest-a-guide-for-charity-trustees-cc29/conflicts-of-interest-a-guide-for-charity-trustees, accessed 4 June 2018.

knowledge or experience. If they do not have particular knowledge, they are expected to take appropriate advice. The Charity Commission also interprets this duty to mean that trustees must be adequately informed in their decision-making. This entails drawing on expert advice where necessary and considering matters in a balanced way.

Outcomes and actions

Many organisations in the voluntary sector are charities, and being a charity makes an organisation subject to a specific set of laws and regulations. Not all charities are registered with the Charity Commission, so if your organisation is a charity this may not be immediately apparent. It is important to understand whether your organisation is a charity, and this chapter should assist you in finding out. You should read this chapter carefully and identify whether your organisation is a charity, and especially whether it should be regulated by the Charity Commission. You should also consider whether you need to take action in relation to any of the laws that apply to charities that are discussed in this chapter.

7 Understanding your constitution

Types of constitution

The constitution of an organisation sets out its purposes, its powers and the rules regarding its governance. Constitutions therefore often cover the same content as each other, no matter the type of organisation to which they belong. However, the type of your organisation will determine the title of its constitution. Table 7.1 shows the titles of the constitutions of various types of organisation.

Depending on the type of organisation, certain legal provisions may affect aspects of the constitution – for example, asset lock requirements for community interest companies (CICs), and charitable purposes and public benefit provisions for charities. Some of these provisions are compulsory, so constitutions must be written in a way that complies with such requirements.

The constitution is the most important document for an organisation. As the secretary it is important that you locate it (the most up-to-date copy), read it and understand it. It is also your role to advise the board on the application of the constitution, what it says and how to operate within it. Boards have legal duties to operate within the constitution of the organisation, and this is particularly the case with charities. While the secretary cannot compel a board to stay within the constitution, it is the secretary's duty to ensure that the board is fully informed of its content.

As mentioned in chapter 5 (see pages 36 and 37), it is possible to create a trust or an unincorporated members' association without any documents, so in some circumstances these types of organisation may not have a written constitution. But this is very rare; it is broadly the case that all types of organisation will have a constitution.

Table 7.1   Titles of constitutions

Legal form	Title of constitution
Trust	Trust Deed, Declaration of Trust, or Charity Commission Scheme
Unincorporated members' association	Rules or Constitution
Company limited by guarantee	Articles (or, for older companies, Memorandum and Articles)
Community interest company	Articles (or, for older companies, Memorandum and Articles)
Community benefit society	Rules
Co-operative society	Rules
Chartered body	Charter (and By-laws)
Charitable incorporated organisation	Constitution

How to locate your current constitution

Where you should look for your current constitution may depend on the legal form of your organisation:

- If your organisation is a registered company, the most up-to-date copy of your constitution should be filed with Companies House. You can search at https://beta.companieshouse.gov.uk for the latest version. If you locate a later version than the copy filed at Companies House, this may mean that the updated version was not filed when it was last amended and you should therefore file it now.
- If your organisation is a registered society, the most up-to-date copy of your constitution should be filed with the Financial Conduct Authority (FCA). You can search at https://mutuals.fsa.gov.uk for the latest version. If you locate a later version than the copy filed at the FCA, this may mean that the updated version was not filed. This will mean that it has not in fact taken effect and you should therefore file it now.
- If your organisation is a registered charity, the most up-to-date copy of your constitution should be filed with the Charity Commission. While

you cannot download it, you can check the date it was last filed by looking under the 'Charity framework' section of your entry in the register of charities (www.gov.uk/find-charity-information). The Charity Commission can send you a copy, but it is advisable that you do all that you can to locate your constitution in other ways before requesting it to be sent. (The Charity Commission will not look very favourably on a charity that is unable to locate its own constitution.)

• In most types of organisation, the constitution is amended by the members. Searching through the papers of members' general meetings should provide you with any changes previously made.

Memorandum and articles of association

In the case of older companies, the constitution was made up of two documents: the memorandum and the articles. Each was a key document, with the memorandum containing more outward-focused details that were difficult to amend (such as the purposes and powers) and the articles being more inwardly focused. If your organisation is a company that pre-dates the Companies Act 2006, your constitution may still take this two-part form.

However, the Companies Act 2006 made significant changes (which took effect in 2009) and the constitution of a company is now simply its articles. For newer companies, the memorandum contains no more than the name of the company and the subscribers (i.e. the people who set it up) – it is not part of the constitution. For older companies, there may still be a memorandum that contains many more sections than this (such as the purposes and powers), but these sections are now considered to be a part of the articles and so should be treated as such.

Content of a constitution

A constitution will typically cover the following details.

Name

The constitution will include the full name of the organisation.

Location

For a company, the articles will state which country the company is registered in. For a community benefit society or a co-operative society, the rules will explicitly include the address of the registered office.

Purposes or objects

Commercial companies no longer have a requirement to have purposes in their articles, but for most voluntary organisations a constitution will include a statement of the organisation's overall purposes – what it is there to do. This is essential if it is a charity. In a charity, the trustees have a legal obligation to ensure that the organisation always operates within these purposes.

Powers

Following on from the purposes, it is common (but not obligatory) to have a section that sets out what the powers of the organisation are – in other words, what it can do in pursuit of its purposes. Companies traditionally listed their powers in their constitution, and many other types of constitution replicate this form.

Non-distribution clause (or asset lock)

A charity will usually have a clause that states that its assets and profits can only be used in pursuit of the purposes and cannot be distributed to members. If your organisation is not a charity, you may not have such a clause, and there is no legal requirement for you to do so. In any case, if your organisation is a not-for-profit, it is likely that there will be such a clause. A key difference between charities and CICs, on the one hand, and other types of voluntary organisation, on the other, is that the other types have the option of varying or removing this clause if they wish. It is very rare for a charity or CIC to be able to do this, but the clause can be altered to some extent with prior consent from the relevant regulator and within the applicable legal rules.

Benefits to members or board members

Linked to the non-distribution clause, a charity – and sometimes other types of organisation – will often have a section setting out which, if any, benefits can be granted to board members or members (see chapter 5, page 49, and chapter 6, page 57).

Conflicts of interest

There are legal requirements with regard to conflicts of interest, for charity trustees (see chapter 6, page 60) and company directors (see chapter 5, page 48). The constitution will often set out how conflicts of interest should be handled, and sometimes when they are allowable.

Limited liability and guarantees

There will be clauses relating to limited liability and guarantees in company articles, in charitable incorporated organisation constitutions, and in community benefit society and co-operative society rules.

Dissolution clause

Sometimes there will be a clause setting out how the organisation can be dissolved or wound up and what should be done with its assets if this happens.

Membership

An organisation that has members (such as an unincorporated members' association or a company) will have a section setting out who the members are, how they are admitted, their rights, any obligations they have, and how and why membership can cease.

Meetings of members

An organisation which has members will have a section containing arrangements for meetings of members. Such meetings are usually called general meetings.

Board

This section will cover who the board members are and how they are appointed, the role of the board and its powers, and arrangements for how the board meets and takes decisions. It is also good practice to include explanations of the board's power to delegate and of the arrangements for setting up committees.

Reporting and regulation

Often there will be a section setting out the requirements for accounting, public reporting, and the records and registers to be kept.

How the constitution can be amended

Sometimes there will be a section setting out how the constitution can be amended. For some types of organisation, such as companies, the way that this can happen is set out in the relevant Acts of Parliament, but there may be more detail added into a constitution. For other types of organisation, such as a non-charitable unincorporated members' association, there are no relevant Acts of Parliament so it is very important that the way the constitution can be amended is set out in the constitution itself.

Model constitutions

There are a number of model constitutions that you can access and use. These include:

- **Charity Commission model constitutions for charities:** These are available via the Charity Commission's website.[1] If you are seeking to set up and register a charity, using a model constitution that the Charity Commission is familiar with can speed things up.

- **Charity Law Association (CLA) model constitution:** The CLA provides a range of excellent model constitutions for unincorporated members' associations, trusts and charitable companies. These can be purchased for £40 (as of the time of writing) and are free for members of the CLA. They are available on the CLA's website.[2]

- **National Housing Federation model rules:** These are suitable for registered providers of social housing that are being set up as community benefit societies.[3]

- **Religious charities:** A number of umbrella groups – such as the National Churches Trust – provide model constitutions.[4]

- **Academies:** The Department for Education provides model articles for academies, and indeed it is a requirement of an academy that it uses this model, with some variation allowed.[5]

- **Sports:** A number of sporting bodies provide model constitutions.

- **CICs:** Model articles are provided by the Office of the Regulator of Community Interest Companies for use when forming or converting to a CIC.[6]

---

[1] See 'Setting up a charity: Model governing documents' [web page], Charity Commission, 2012, www.gov.uk/government/publications/setting-up-a-charity-model-governing-documents, accessed 6 June 2018.

[2] See 'Model documents' [web page], Charity Law Association, 2018, https://charitylawassociation.org.uk/model-documents, accessed 8 June 2018.

[3] See 'Model rules 2015' [web page], National Housing Federation, 2015, www.housing.org.uk/resource-library/browse/model-rules-2015, accessed 8 June 2018.

[4] See 'Resources – governance' [web page], National Churches Trust, 2018, www.nationalchurchestrust.org/churches-trusts-forum/resources, accessed 8 June 2018.

[5] See 'Model articles of association for academy trusts' [web page], Department for Education, 2017, www.gov.uk/government/publications/academy-model-memorandum-and-articles-of-association, accessed 8 June 2018.

[6] See 'Community interest companies: Model constitutions' [web page], Office of

- **Co-operatives:** Co-operatives UK provides a range of model constitutions for co-operatives.[7]

Company model articles

It is important to realise that, if your organisation is a company, there are model articles that will apply to you as a default. There is a range of model articles authorised by Parliament. There are different models for different types of company (such as private share companies and private companies limited by guarantee). These articles can be found at www.gov.uk/guidance/model-articles-of-association-for-limited-companies. Under company law, these model articles apply as a default unless a company has adopted alternative wording or unless the company's articles expressly excludes them. This means that if there is a gap in your articles, the relevant provision of these model articles could be deemed to apply. For example, if your articles fail to say how directors (board members) are appointed, then the relevant sections of the model articles will apply.

These model articles can be quite useful for people who want to set up a company very quickly, as upon incorporation as a company it is possible to simply tick a box saying that you will adopt the model articles. The articles can sometimes also be useful for subsidiary companies.

However, it does need to be noted that the model articles for companies limited by guarantee are not designed for not-for-profit companies and in some instances may not be suitable for the needs of such companies. In addition, the model articles are not appropriate for charities, so it is probably a good idea for charitable companies to include a clause in their constitution expressly excluding the model articles. This could be worded as follows: 'The relevant model articles for a company limited by guarantee are hereby expressly excluded.'

Amendment of a constitution

It is quite likely that, in the process of reading this book, you will begin to understand your own constitution better and perhaps even look at some of the models that are available. In this way, you might reach the conclusion that your constitution needs to be amended.

the Regulator of Community Interest Companies, 2017, www.gov.uk/government/publications/community-interest-companies-constitutions, accessed 8 June 2018.

[7] See 'Model governing documents' [web page], Co-operatives UK, 2018, www.uk.coop/developing-co-ops/model-governing-documents, accessed 8 June 2018.

Whether you have the power to amend your constitution (and how this can be done) will depend on the legal form your organisation takes. Table 7.2 sets out the standard processes for amending a constitution.

If your organisation is a registered charity, you will often need the consent of the Charity Commission to make changes to your constitution. What will require consent will depend on your charity's legal form. However, if consent is required, it must be received prior to making the change. Therefore, if the change needs to be voted on by the charity's members before taking effect, you will need the Charity Commission's consent before putting the matter to your members.

Table 7.2 Powers to amend a constitution

Type of organisation	Constitutional provisions	Who can amend	Statutory powers surrounding amendments
Trust	The trust deed may give the trustees power of amendment. Note: if your organisation is a charity, prior approval from the Charity Commission will be required for some changes (see below) and the deed itself may require the Charity Commission to approve other amendments. Prior approval by the Charity Commission is required for: • any change to the purposes (unless the organisation has a gross income of less than £10,000 and certain conditions are met); • any change regarding spending money or disposing of land held as a permanent endowment; • paying a trustee or connected person; • awarding third parties rights to nominate trustees or take part in decisions.	Usually the trustees amend the trust deed.	The Charities Act 2011 gives the trustees of an unincorporated charity an express power of amendment for any administrative power or administrative procedures. This power only applies to charities. Also, it cannot be used to change the purposes, to provide benefits to trustees, or to change the rights of other parties to nominate trustees. If the organisation is a charity and it had a gross income of £10,000 or less in the previous year, the Charities Act 2011 also gives it the power to amend its purposes provided certain conditions are met. In addition, a charitable trust can apply to the Charity Commission to make amendments.

Type of organisation	Constitutional provisions	Who can amend	Statutory powers surrounding amendments
Unincorporated members' association	The rules may include a power to amend the constitution. Note: if your organisation is a charity, prior approval from the Charity Commission will be required for some changes (see below) and the rules themselves may require the Charity Commission to approve other amendments. Prior approval by the Charity Commission is required for: • any change to the purposes (unless the organisation has a gross income of less than £10,000 and certain conditions are met); • any change on spending money or disposing of land held as permanent endowment; • paying a trustee or connected person; • awarding third parties rights to nominate trustees or take part in decisions.	Usually it is the members who need to approve any change.	Same as for trusts (above).
Company limited by guarantee	The power of amendment is set out in the Companies Act 2006, but the wording of this is sometimes replicated in the articles, and the articles may include additional provisions (such as in cases where additional approval is required). Note: if your organisation is a charity, prior approval from the Charity Commission will be required for some changes (see below) and the articles themselves may require the Charity Commission to approve other amendments. Charity Commission prior approval is required for: • any change to the objects/purposes; • what can happen to the charity's property when it is wound up; • paying a trustee or connected person.	Members	The Companies Act 2006 specifies that the members of a company may amend the articles by passing a special resolution to do so (see chapter 10). Amendments to articles have to be filed with Companies House (see chapter 12) and any amendment to the purposes is not effective until it has been filed.

Type of organisation	Constitutional provisions	Who can amend	Statutory powers surrounding amendments
Community interest company	The power of amendment is set out in the Companies Act 2006, but the wording of this is sometimes replicated in the articles, and the articles may include additional provisions (such as in cases where additional approval is required). Note: for a CIC, there are some clauses in the articles (e.g. the asset lock clause) which are statutory requirements and so cannot be removed or altered without prior consent from the CIC Regulator.	Members	Same as for companies limited by guarantee (above).
Community benefit society or co-operative society	The rules will usually include a provision on how they can be amended.	Members	The Co-operative and Community Benefit Societies Act 2014 sets out how rules can be amended. Rule changes have to be filed with the Financial Conduct Authority before they take effect.
Chartered body	The procedures for amendment are usually included within the charter. A chartered body's charter and by-laws can only be amended with the agreement of the Privy Council. Note: if your organisation is a charity, Charity Commission approval is required for some changes and the charter and by-laws themselves may require the Charity Commission to approve broader amendments.	Depends on the organisation	Not applicable.

Type of organisation	Constitutional provisions	Who can amend	Statutory powers surrounding amendments
Charitable incorporated organisation	The procedure for amendment will usually be included in the constitution and is included in the models provided by the Charity Commission. Prior approval by the Charity Commission will be required for some changes (see below) and the constitution itself may require the Charity Commission to approve other amendments. Charity Commission prior approval is required for: • any change to the objects/purposes; • what can happen to the charity's property when it is wound up; • paying a trustee or connected person. Furthermore, an amendment (of any kind) will not take effect until it has been registered with the Charity Commission.	Members	Not applicable.

Outcomes and actions

After reading this chapter you should understand:
• why your organisation has a constitution;
• how to locate it;
• what information it will usually contain;
• how to amend it.

As secretary, you should locate and read your organisation's constitution. You should also have a look at the typical contents of relevant model constitutions and consider whether there are any gaps in your constitution or any sections that may need to be updated or amended.

8 Who does what in an organisation?

Board members

Every organisation will have a governing group that takes overall responsibility for its work. This group may have any of a number of different titles – typical descriptions are the board, the trustees, the management committee, the executive committee, the governors and the council. Essentially, references to the board mean the group of people who have general control of your organisation and who are responsible for its management and administration. They may be different from the people who are responsible for *carrying out* that management and administration, as a larger organisation will employ staff and delegate to them. But the board retains primary responsibility and is ultimately responsible for all of the acts of the organisation. It is responsible for ensuring that the organisation is effective, is properly run and is meeting its overall purposes as set out in its constitution.

Board members are key to the work of an organisation and the role of the board secretary. Much of the work of the board secretary is concerned with supporting the board and enabling it to work effectively. The other reason why board members are so important is that, as alluded to in the previous paragraph, they carry the legal responsibility for the organisation. In an incorporated body, board members have limited liability. However, they still have legal duties, and if they breach their duties then liabilities may arise. An explanation of the duties of board members is set out in chapter 5, with further information covered on pages 144 to 145.

Although voluntary organisations can take on any of a number of forms of various sizes and structures, the work of the board is fundamentally the same across all types of organisation.

Sometimes there can be a lack of clarity about who exactly the board members are. There may be a wide group of people who attend your board meetings, and their individual functions may not always be clear. If your organisation is a company, your board members are your company directors, and they should all be listed on the register of companies held at

Companies House (see www.gov.uk/get-information-about-a-company). If your organisation is a registered charity, your board members should be listed as trustees on the register of charities (see www.gov.uk/find-charity-information). Note that, if your organisation is a charitable company, it will be listed on both websites. However, these listings may not always be up to date and accurate. If you are unclear about who your board members are, you can:

- **Check your constitution:** This should tell you the overall size of your board and how they are appointed. You may also have some board members who hold their position ex officio (i.e. by virtue of holding another role), and if so your constitution should provide details.
- **Check past minutes:** Your constitution will tell you how the board is appointed. If the board appoints its own members, check through the minutes of past board meetings to see who was appointed and when. If the members appoint the board, check through the minutes of the general meetings.
- **Check your registers:** Many types of charity have a requirement to hold a register of board members and/or directors. If you have such a register, check it. This is particularly important in a company where entry on a register of directors is held to be proof that somebody is a director.
- **Consider what people's roles are in a board meeting:** In any meeting, you will usually find that there are board members, people in attendance (usually staff or advisers) and sometimes observers. It is only the actual members of the board who are entitled to vote on a matter. While others may contribute to a discussion, they should not take part in the decision-making. Having said this, these roles are not always completely evident or understood at meetings. You could seek to address this by having all attendees sign in, and also listing their role, but if you do this try to ensure that you have another way of checking that they have listed their role correctly.

Although a board is responsible for everything, for it to work effectively it should try to function at a strategic level and not get too involved in operational detail. Your board's ability to do this will vary to some extent depending on the size of your organisation – in smaller organisations, boards may be more involved in day-to-day issues. There is more on this in chapter 15.

Another important point about board members is that the board is a collective decision-making body. An individual board member has no authority to act on behalf of the organisation, unless the board has delegated such authority to that particular individual.

Members

Depending on your legal form, you may have members. This means members in the legal sense: people who have rights under your constitution and/or the laws governing your type of organisation. You may have groupings of supporters that you call members, in the same way that some organisation have 'friends'. Think about this group and whether they do in fact have any formal rights as members. Can they attend and vote at general meetings? Is it they who amend your constitution? Do they appoint board members?

People who are members in the legal sense will have particular rights, and in some cases duties, depending on your legal form.

Trusts

A trust does not usually have members – a trust deed will generally just refer to the role of trustees. Therefore, if you are a trust and have members, your members will probably just be an informal membership group.

Unincorporated members' associations

By virtue of its name, you can see that this type of legal entity has members. Their rights and responsibilities are set out in the constitution.

Companies limited by guarantee and community interest companies

As both of these types of legal entity are companies, they must have at least one member (as outlined in chapter 5, pages 38–41). The members could just be the board members of the organisation wearing a different hat, or your organisation could have appointed a wider group of people as members. The Companies Act 2006 confers a number of statutory rights on members:

- right to attend and vote at general meetings;
- right to appoint a proxy;
- right to remove directors;
- right to appoint auditors;
- right to convene a general meeting;
- right to amend the articles.

Charitable incorporated organisations

In the same way that a company must have at least one member, so must a charitable incorporated organisation (CIO). The members may just be the trustees, such as in a foundation CIO, or there may be a broader membership, as in an association CIO. The Charities Act 2011 places a duty on a CIO's members:

> Each member of a CIO must exercise the powers that the member has in that capacity in the way that the member decides, in good faith, would be most likely to further the purposes of the CIO.[1]

However, the legislation for CIOs does not define the powers of the members in the same way as the Companies Act 2006 does, although it does state that the constitution of a CIO must include provisions about who is eligible for membership and how to become a member.[2] In addition, the CIO (General) Regulations 2012 state that a CIO's constitution must include certain 'standard member provisions' relating to membership and the holding of general meetings.[3] The model constitutions provided by the Charity Commission contain all of these rights, and in many ways these constitutions provide that a CIO member has very similar rights to those of a company member.

Honorary officers

Honorary officers are the voluntary officers of an organisation. They are people who take on specific roles, usually on an unpaid basis. They are usually also board members, but this is not always the case. In some instances, individuals take on the role of treasurer without also being on the board. In addition, if an organisation has an honorary secretary, this person is also sometimes not a board member. The most common honorary officer roles are chair, vice-chair (or deputy chair), treasurer and secretary. These roles may be provided for in your constitution, which may also set out how the roles are appointed. This means that they may be optional or they may be required. It is important to remember that

---

[1] 'Charities Act 2011' [web page], UK Government, 2011, www.legislation.gov.uk/ukpga/2011/25/section/220, Section 220, accessed 20 April 2018.

[2] 'Charities Act 2011' [web page], UK Government, 2011, www.legislation.gov.uk/ukpga/2011/25/section/206, Section 206, accessed 20 April 2018.

[3] 'Charitable Incorporated Organisations (General) Regulations 2012' [web page], UK Government, 2012, www.legislation.gov.uk/uksi/2012/3012/regulation/13/made, Section 13(3), accessed 20 April 2018.

these roles have no specific powers or duties beyond what the board or a constitution gives to them, and so there is no need for them to be referred to in a constitution for an appointment to be made. This means that if your board wishes to appoint a treasurer, it can do so without a power being set out in the constitution.

Chair

The chair will be a board member whose primary role is to chair meetings of the board. Of all the honorary officer roles, it is the one most likely to be referred to in the constitution. The constitution will usually set out how the chair is elected or appointed. The most common method is for this appointment to be made by the board itself and for the chair to be appointed from the pool of existing board members. However, sometimes a board will externally appoint a chair, bringing somebody onto the board from outside the organisation to take on this role. In addition, in some membership organisations it is the members who appoint, or elect, this role directly.

While the primary role of this position is to chair meetings of the board, most chairs will take on a number of additional responsibilities. The chair of the board will usually also chair general meetings, and the constitution may give the chair specific powers in regard to this role (sometimes it gives them a casting vote, a power to call for poll votes or a power to adjourn meetings). The role of chairing the board meetings usually extends beyond the actual meetings themselves, with the chair taking on a role in managing the effective functioning of the board.

Typically, a chair will be responsible for undertaking the ongoing supervision and management of the chief executive on behalf of the board. The chief executive will report to the full board, but it is usually the chair who deals with the relationship on a day-to-day basis – holding performance reviews, setting targets, and agreeing leave and expenses.

The chair should also oversee the effective running of the board – agreeing agendas and sometimes reviewing papers before circulation – and will take the lead on board governance. This involves looking at performance reviews, undertaking one-to-one meetings, resolving conflicts on the board, undertaking skills assessments, conducting succession planning, and arranging inductions and training (see chapters 14 and 15).

The chair will often represent the organisation and act as a figurehead. In some organisations, the chair will also have some authority to take decisions on operational matters (e.g. where the board wants some type of board member agreement) or will review urgent matters that arise between meetings.

The role of the chair is often perceived as having a great deal of authority. While this may be true, it is important to remember that a board acts collectively and that no single board member has authority unless this has been delegated by the board. This applies to the chair in the same way as it applies to other board members. So, while all of the aforementioned duties are common for a chair, the chair will need to be assigned these duties by the board. The chair does not have the authority to act unless the board gives it to them. The chair is a role where it is vital to have a clear role profile and/or job description.

Vice-chair (or deputy chair)

Many organisations also have a vice-chair. This role may be a requirement of the constitution and the means of election or appointment may be provided for in the constitution – but not necessarily. The nature of the role can vary, but essentially the purpose of a vice-chair is to act as the chair when the chair is absent and to assist the chair with their duties. There may be more than one vice-chair, and in some organisations the role is seen as a chair-elect (which effectively means the vice-chair will become the chair when the current chair ends their tenure). This can often be an informal assumption, with no automatic right to move from one role to the next. It can also be a presumption that can cause conflict on the board, if a vice-chair sees themselves as a chair in waiting and is challenged by the board or by another board member.

It can be quite difficult to draft a role profile and/or job description for a vice-chair, as often it involves no more than stepping into the role of the chair when necessary. To define the role more clearly, ask questions such as: are there some duties of the chair that you would not expect the vice-chair to undertake? Is the role of the chair really perceived as solely relating to the chairing of meetings? If you have assigned specific roles to the vice-chair, remember that these must be explicitly authorised by the board and/or delegated to the vice-chair.

Treasurer

The treasurer is a board member or volunteer with specific responsibilities regarding the organisation's finances. These can relate purely to scrutiny, with the board asking someone with financial experience to undertake a detailed review on its behalf and then report back. Sometimes, particularly in smaller organisations, the treasurer may have delegated authority surrounding financial approvals. This role may be a requirement of the constitution and the means of election or appointment may also (but not necessarily) be provided for in the constitution.

The work of the treasurer can vary significantly but some typical roles are:

- reviewing the management accounts and financial reports on behalf of the board, then reporting back;
- presenting annual accounts to the members;
- chairing a finance committee;
- advising the board on how to carry out its financial responsibilities;
- especially in smaller organisations, taking on some operational financial duties, such as budgeting, signing cheques and preparing reports.

When discussing the responsibilities of a treasurer, it is important that the board members fully understand that a treasurer has no higher level of duty than they do as a board member. The board members have equal responsibility for the finances of the organisation, and having a treasurer does not relieve them of that responsibility in any way. It is arguable that in some instances having a treasurer can put an organisation at risk of having a board that does not fully scrutinise financial matters as a collective body, as it should. In addition, if yours is a larger body with a finance staff and a finance manager, you may want to consider whether you still need this role. If you have a finance committee, the primary role of the treasurer may be to chair that committee, and so chair of the finance committee may be a more appropriate title.

Presidents and patrons

Many organisations appoint patrons, presidents or vice-presidents. These terms are usually used to denote people who act as figureheads and support the organisation. They may be celebrities who are happy to lend their name to the charity, members of the royal family or people with expertise in the work of the organisation. For example, the National Garden Scheme has Mary Berry as its president; she is an appropriate figure for the role because, as well as being a very well-known celebrity, she opened her garden for the National Garden Scheme for over 20 years. Presidents and patrons are essentially high-level volunteers – these roles are primarily about lending support. It is less common for the roles to have any specific duties or to be involved in the governance of the organisation, unless this is provided for in the constitution.

Whether or not they have *general* duties or responsibilities, patrons and presidents usually have no *legal* duties or responsibilities – they are not board members, unless the constitution provides that they are. In professional bodies, the president is usually a board member, but this is a different situation – it is just that the term president is used to refer to the chair of the board.

Some constitutions refer to the roles of presidents and patrons (or similar roles), setting out how they can be appointed and sometimes the criteria for their appointment. However, because these roles are usually figurehead roles only, there is no need for them to be referred to in the constitution. A board does not need to have a specific power to appoint such roles.

Problems occur when there is a lack of clarity and no consistency over why people have been appointed. While an organisation will usually only have one president, it can have a number of patrons and often has a number of vice-presidents. It can often happen that an organisation ends up with a list of names and no full understanding or agreement as to each person's role or their term of office. Sometimes the people on the list will have fallen out of contact with the organisation. It can even be the case that, when organisations are reviewing long lists of vice-presidents or supporters that have developed over time, it is discovered that those lists still contain supporters who have in fact passed away.

Advice does exist, however, to help you to manage these roles:

- Where you can, appoint people to a role for a set term of office – perhaps three or five years. This can be renewable. However, if you make it clear to the volunteer at the time of their appointment that there is a term of office, this provides you with an opportunity to go back to them periodically and for you both to assess how the appointment is working. You can also end the relationship easily at the end of a term of office, if need be.

- In some cases you will need to make appointments on a permanent or ongoing basis. This is particularly the case with royal appointments.

- Think about the terminology that you use and whether you are giving the person the best title. While these roles will not usually have formal responsibilities, there are common understandings of the various titles, so the public will expect certain titles to mean certain things. A president is perceived to be the head of an organisation, vice-presidents are considered to be of lesser importance and patrons are assumed to be supporters only.

- Even if post-holders have a limited role, it is a good idea to be clear about what you expect the role to be. You should clearly set out your expectations of presidents, vice-presidents and patrons. A role profile or job description can be drafted and shared.

- Be realistic in your expectations. Post-holders will often have a fairly low level of involvement and may undertake the role for a number of organisations.
- Your organisation should be very clear about why it is appointing to these roles and what the benefits are. Is it to lend high-profile support? Or to open doors to you and help you to network? Sometimes, there will be no clear ongoing benefit – you may simply choose to use a title such as vice-president to honour people who have contributed to the work of the organisation. Sometimes it is a way of maintaining contact with and retaining the support of outgoing board members or honorary officers. This is fine, and it is a common way of using these roles – but the board should be clear with itself about whether it is appointing for this reason and about its ongoing expectations (if any) of the post-holder.

Outcomes and actions

This chapter has set out the various high-level roles in an organisation. As secretary, you need to be clear about who does what. It could be an idea to sit down now and list:

- who your organisation's board members are;
- who your organisation's members are (if it should have members);
- who your organisation's honorary officers are; and
- who your organisations president, vice-president and/or patrons are (if applicable).

You might also want to think about whether they all have an understanding of their respective roles. Does your organisation have role descriptions of board members and honorary officers? Should they be updated?

9 Delegation

The board is the main cog in running a successful organisation, but it cannot do everything and it cannot take every decision. It has to delegate – meaning it has to ask others, or individual members of the board, to do things on its behalf. That said, a board always retains responsibility for all of the decisions and actions that are taken on its behalf. A board cannot wash its hands of the responsibly once it is delegated. It therefore needs to know how each decision or action has been carried out. Has the action already been taken? Were there any difficulties? Are there any changes that need to be made?

As an example, think about when a board agrees a budget for the forthcoming year. Would it seem acceptable to you for it to agree the budget and not consider it again until the end of the year? That would not be a board operating effectively. Instead, the board should receive regular reports on how the budget is being spent throughout the year. The board should consider whether some things have gone over budget, whether there are some areas where much less money has been spent than planned, and whether any of these circumstances have highlighted difficulties. It should also review whether the organisation's income is as expected. Boards need to engage in monitoring activity on a regular basis.

There are three key things to consider in regard to delegation:
* Delegation should be **appropriate**.
* Delegation should be **clear**.
* Delegation should be **monitored**.

When considering delegation, think about how appropriate it is. Is the matter to be delegated really too big a decision to be handed over, and should the board itself take the decision? Alternatively, think about whether the board is being too reluctant to let go of certain matters. It might be that the board is operating in far too operational a manner.

Matters reserved by the board

There are some decisions which are so large, or so fundamental to the role of the board, that they should never be delegated. The board is always responsible for setting the strategy and direction of the organisation and so there are certain decisions that it must always take. If the board is setting the strategy, this means that it is the board that will need to give final approval of any strategic plan or strategy. Linked to this, it will also need to agree the business plan and budget for the organisation each year. Board members have a legal duty to exercise reasonable levels of skill and care, and delegating decisions on matters such as these would be a sign that a board was not exercising the required level of care.

There are also some statutory requirements of a board, depending on the type of organisation. For example, the annual report and accounts must be signed off by the board each year and they have to contain the date that sign-off was provided. This means that they have to be agreed by the board – this approval cannot be delegated. In addition, some regulators place requirements on boards to consider certain matters and not to delegate them. Finally, there will be crucial decisions which the board considers to carry too high a risk to be delegated.

The board should be clear about which matters it will never delegate – often called 'matters reserved by the board'. It is best practice for the board to agree a list of all such matters. There are a number of model lists available (from various sources) which are used across all sectors. ICSA: The Governance Institute provides a model, but this is only available to its members. Co-operatives UK provides a model called 'Matters Reserved for the Board'.[1]

Typically, the types of matter reserved by the board will include:

- approval of the strategy or corporate plan, and any statements regarding vision, mission or values;
- approval of the annual plan and any business plans, and of the annual budget;
- approval of any matters of significant risk outside the agreed business plan and budget;
- approval of the annual report and accounts;
- approval of committee terms of reference and appointments to committees;
- approval of the risk management policy and the overall amount of risk that the organisation is willing to take (risk appetite);
- appointment of the chief executive;
- appointment of the secretary.

---

[1] *Matters reserved for the board* [PDF], Co-operatives UK, 2018, www.uk.coop/ sites/default/files/uploads/attachments/matters_reserved_for_the_board.pdf, accessed 6 June 2018.

While there are model lists that you can use, it is probably best to use only one of these as a starting point and then to move on from there. Getting your board to agree its list of matters reserved is a very good way of getting it to begin to look at its own method of working. It may be that once your board starts to discuss this topic, you find that different board members have different approaches to delegation and that some are much more prepared to delegate than others.

The other helpful thing about agreeing this list is that it can then feed into your work planning for the board. If your board decides that it will agree an annual business plan and budget for the executive to work within, you will need to begin to plan for when in the year this will need to be approved, when any updates to the plan will be considered (if this is allowable), and how and when it will be monitored.

Clarity of delegation

Another reason for asking your board to begin to consider its list of matters reserved is that this is a very good starting point for getting clarity about what the level of delegation will be. In many voluntary organisations, the level of delegation is not clearly documented and there are sometimes a number of unspoken assumptions about what can be, and is, delegated. You might think that a chief executive would be the first person to want clarity with regard to delegation. However, if an organisation has developed a set of unwritten practices around delegation which have never really been formally acknowledged, the chief executive may be reluctant to put those practices down on paper. One scenario in which this could be the case is if the organisation is about to enter into a large contract under the assumed practices of delegation, without challenge by the board. If the board is then asked whether they are happy to formally agree to that level of delegation, they may begin to question it.

That said, delegations do need to be formally recorded. Without a clear record, the person who has been delegated to is placing themselves at risk. If things go wrong, there will be no way of them showing that they were acting with authority. The board also will not be able to show that it was exercising reasonable skill and care. Finally, when delegations are undocumented, the result can be some real inconsistencies across the organisation, with some areas or staff members exercising a very high level of authority and others needing to refer everything back up to the board. This can lead to a very ineffective way of working for the organisation and the board.

The board therefore needs to be recording its delegations as well as showing who is being given authority and what the level of authority is (including whether there are financial boundaries on the decisions that can be made). How the board documents its delegations will vary, but having a list of matters reserved for the board is a good starting point. The list could then just state that all other decisions are delegated to the chief executive. However, this may be too simple a statement for many organisations. Furthermore, if the board has committees that are not just advisory, delegations will be made not only to the chief executive but also to the committees. There may also be occasions when there are delegations to individual board members, such as the chair or treasurer.

The delegations can be set out in various ways.

Constitution

Many constitutions say that day-to-day administration is delegated to a chief executive but do not define day-to-day administration. Greater clarity can then be provided in the chief executive's job description.

Role descriptions

If the board has honorary officers who have delegated powers, these powers should be made clear in their role descriptions. Delegations may also be specified in staff job descriptions.

Committee terms of reference

If a board is delegating power to a committee, this should be specified in the terms of reference, and the details of the delegation should be explicitly listed in those terms. Sometimes a list of the functions or purposes of a committee can fail to make it clear whether the committee is just an advisory group or whether it has the authority to take decisions.

Annual business plan and budget

When a board agrees to an annual business plan and budget for staff to work within, this can sometimes be seen as an agreement to delegate. However, it should always be made explicit whether the agreement to the plan itself also gives staff delegated authority to carry out actions within that plan. Usually, authority is implied – for example, agreeing the salary budget for the year generally grants authority to pay those salaries. However, there are often some key items within a budget where the expectation is that they will be brought back to the board for further agreement. Two examples of this are pay awards (a figure may be set aside in the budget but the board may want to give specific approval) and capital expenditure. There is nothing wrong with reserving approval in this way, but the board must make its intentions regarding authority to act and delegation very clear.

Policies

Boards will often agree policies that set out delegations within them. For example, the risk management policy, which must be agreed by the board, will usually give day-to-day management of operational risks to staff. The board may also agree HR policies that give authority to the chief executive or head of HR, and financial policies tend to contain a range of delegations.

Minutes

You may be able to record specific delegations in the board minutes, either for one-off items or in areas where more clarity is needed.

It is normal for delegations to arise in all of these ways, but this can make it difficult for people to put their finger on exactly who is authorised to do what. It is a good idea to have one summary document that lists all delegations together. This is commonly called a 'scheme of delegation' or a 'schedule of delegation', and an example format is set out in table 9.1.

Once a board has decided what it will never delegate as well as what it will delegate and to whom, it must consider how it will monitor actions that are taken on its behalf. Board meetings are generally used to consider significant decisions or policy matters that require the full board's consideration, but it is also usually necessary to spend some time considering reports from staff and committees on delegated matters. Your board will need to determine how best it can monitor these matters and agree the format for these reports.

Table 9.1 Scheme of delegation: example content and format

	Board	Committees	Management
Strategy	Reviews and determines the mission, values, strategy and objectives. Approves overall policies and plans, at a high level, to achieve strategic objectives.		Chief executive advises the board on strategic issues requiring debate and approval. Chief executive implements agreed strategy.
Business plan and budget	Approves annual business plan and budget.	Finance Committee reviews draft budget and makes recommendations to the board.	Chief executive presents the business plan and budget to the board for approval. Chief executive implements business plan and budget.
Acquisition and authorisation of goods and services	Approves all items over £x (in total) or outside budget and business plan, or items that are not the direct consequence of a board decision.		Chief executive has authority up to £x, in accordance with the budget and business plan, or in direct consequence of a board decision. All authority limits below this to be set out in the Financial Procedures. All decisions to be made in accordance with the rules on tendering and quotes.

	Board	Committees	Management
Other policy matters	Approves all policy matters that may involve significant financial or other risk, or that raise significant issues of principle. Sets a policy framework at a high level.	Committees advise the board on policy in their respective areas.	Chief executive is responsible for drawing the attention of the board to major policy issues. Executive team is responsible for approving policies, within the policy framework agreed by the board.
Risk	Overall responsibility for risk management. Sets risk policy. Agrees risk appetite.	Audit Committee is responsible for reviewing the risk management process.	Management is responsible for identifying, controlling and managing risks in their own areas. Management is also responsible for co-ordinating risk management. activities, including reporting to the Audit Committee and board.
Recruitment and selection of staff	Approves overall budget for staff as part of business plan. Approves the appointment or removal of the chief executive.	Nominations Committee approves the appointment or removal of executive directors.	Chief executive is responsible for the recruitment of all other staff within the budget and business plan.

Approved by the board on [*insert date here*].

Outcomes and actions

After reading this chapter, you should understand why it is important that there is clarity about:

- the role of the board;
- what the board delegates;
- what decisions the board thinks that it must always take.

Think about your own organisation and whether there are clear delegations. Has the board listed the matters that it thinks it should always consider? Is there clarity about what other decisions are delegated? Have a look at the example scheme of delegation set out in table 9.1 and consider whether there is clear understanding across your own organisation about who takes which decisions.

10 Meetings

Before considering meetings and decision-making, you should consider the glossary of commonly used terms set out in table 10.1.

Table 10.1   Terminology of meetings

Term	Definition
Casting vote	Following a vote, if there is a tie the chair can vote again and thereby determine the outcome. Note that a casting vote is a second vote; having this right does not prevent a chair from voting the first time. A chair only has a casting vote if this right is contained in the constitution.
Abstain	This means choosing not to vote. Abstentions usually do not count when considering the number of votes cast (for the exception, see 'Unanimous' below). In addition, a person does not need to say that they are abstaining for it to be an abstention – just choosing not to vote is enough.
Unanimous	A unanimous vote is one where everyone entitled to vote votes in favour (although it is just as possible to unanimously vote against something, the term is less often used in this way). In this instance, it is not just that nobody votes against the matter; there also need to be no abstentions.
Resolution	An official decision that is made by a group, usually after a vote is taken. See chapter 11 for more detailed information on resolutions.

Term	Definition
Ordinary resolution	A resolution that can be passed by a simple majority (meaning just over 50% of votes cast).
Special resolution	Some matters, such as the amendment of a constitution, typically require a higher majority than a simple majority. These are called special resolutions. In company law, a special resolution requires a 75% majority of votes cast (when the matter is dealt with in a meeting).
Written resolution	An official decision made by a group when the voting was conducted in writing (which can include email communication, if this is within the relevant legal rules) rather than at a meeting.
Proxy	A proxy is a person who is appointed by a member to attend a meeting on their behalf and to vote. In company law, there is a statutory right to appoint any person as a proxy, and proxies have statutory rights.
Notice	This term is usually employed in regard to general meetings. It is a notification, sent to members, setting out the time, place and date of a general meeting. It also needs to contain the business that will be considered at the meeting, including the wording of resolutions being proposed. In company law, there are legal requirements regarding other matters that must appear on the notice (such as information about proxy voting).
Clear days'	Clear days' notice means that you do not include the date that notice was deemed to be served and you do not include the date of the meeting. This means that, for example, 14 clear days' notice is in fact 16 days.

Term	Definition
Quorum	The minimum number of members who must be present to enable a meeting to be valid and to proceed.
Unanimity principle	The unanimity principle is a common-law principle that if a decision is taken unanimously it does not matter how the decision was taken; it is still valid. This is a principle that applies in many jurisdictions, and in the UK it is also referred to as the 'Duomatic principle', which refers specially to decisions of shareholders. In the case of *Re Duomatic Ltd* [1969] 2 Ch. 365, the judge summarised the principle as follows: Where it can be shown that all shareholders who have a right to attend and vote at a general meeting of the company assent to some matter which a general meeting of the company could carry into effect, that assent is as binding as a resolution in general meeting would be.[1] While this refers to shareholders' decisions (in other words, the decisions of members), the principle is also usually considered to apply to unanimous decisions of board members. In this way, it allows a unanimous decision to be taken by a board by written resolution, even if there is no power to take a decision by written resolution in the constitution.

Meetings are a fundamental part of the operation of an organisation. Your organisation will have a board, and a key fact about boards is that they are collective decision-making bodies. Being appointed as a board member

---

[1] 'Jordans FAQs: What is the "Duomatic principle" & why is it important?' [web page], AccountingWeb, 2014, www.accountingweb.co.uk/community/industry-insights/jordans-faqs-what-is-the-duomatic-principle-why-is-it-important, accessed 1 November 2017.

does not empower an individual with authority unless the board delegates it to them. Boards take decisions collectively, by coming together. While there are clearly some voluntary organisations that are originally set up by strong-minded individuals, each organisation should eventually reach the stage where it needs to start operating as a group. If a cycle of board meetings (with meetings occurring at least quarterly) is not part of the usual operations of your organisation, this is an indication that there are likely to be some governance concerns. If a board is not meeting regularly enough, this implies that the board members are not in a position to reach collective decisions and that someone is making decisions individually.

As board secretary, organising and attending meetings will be a key part of your role and you will spend quite a bit of your time thinking about them. The three types of meeting that a secretary will need to attend and advise on are:

- general meetings (of members);
- board meetings;
- committee meetings.

There are quite a lot of legal requirements for meetings. This chapter begins by outlining some of the principles, as this should help you to understand why certain laws and rules apply as well as how the principles apply to your meetings. Generally, the legal requirements for these types of meeting will be covered by your constitution and common law. There is far less statutory regulation of board and committee meetings than of general meetings of members, as there is considerable regulation of general meetings in charitable incorporated organisations (CIOs), community interest companies (CICs) and other companies.

What makes a meeting valid?

What is meant by 'meeting'? How is this term defined? Or, to put it another way, if a decision needs to be taken by a board, what do you need to do to ensure that the decision is validly taken?

It has been determined by the courts that a valid meeting normally consists of people who can both see and hear each other (this was decided in *Byng v London Life Association* [1989] 1 All ER 560). This definition of a meeting applies unless a constitution allows for another definition. This default definition means that a meeting needs to be held either with everybody in the same place or by videoconference. It means that teleconferencing (in other words, with audio only) does not constitute a meeting unless the constitution provides for this. This strict definition could cause difficulties for many organisations, as holding meetings by teleconference is common (either with everyone on the telephone or with most of the participants coming together and some people ringing in). For this reason, it is best practice for the constitution of a voluntary organisation to explicitly allow its boards and committees to meet in this way, as illustrated in the following example.

Constitution: example wording for the definition of meetings

A meeting of the board may be held either in person or by suitable electronic means agreed by the board in which all participants may communicate with all the other participants.

Another thing that needs to be considered is that, with the exception of a company that only has one member, a meeting must consist of at least two people. This may seem like an obvious point, but this is one of several other principles that you need to consider to ensure that a meeting is valid. Three of these – giving notice, ensuring that the notice is sufficient and provides the necessary information, and ensuring there are enough members for a decision to be valid – are considered in the following sections. The sections consider each of these principles in regard to one type of meeting: a board meeting.

Giving notice to participants

All of the participants need to be aware of the meeting. The term that is used here is always 'notice'. A decision taken at a meeting is normally considered to be invalid if some of the board members who would have had a right to take part were excluded from the meeting or were not made aware of it.

All board members have the right to receive notice of a meeting. Notice should be given to all board members, even if you know that some of them cannot attend or if they ask you not to give them notice. Notice of board meetings does not need to be given in writing unless this is a requirement of your constitution. However, giving notice in writing means that you have clear evidence that fair notice was given.

Giving sufficient notice and information

Notice must also be reasonable. Participants need to be informed of a meeting far enough in advance, and they need to be told what will be considered at the meeting. What is considered to be reasonable notice depends on the circumstances, but if you work on the principle of giving at least seven days' notice of a meeting this should be sufficient. Even if it is not possible to provide a detailed agenda, board members should be informed of what the business of the meeting is going to be. It is also important to avoid any suggestion of the notice having being misleading, such as telling board members that one matter of business will be considered and then going on to discuss another.

Ensuring there are enough board members to make a decision valid

There are two elements to ensuring there are enough board members to make a decision valid:

* whether a sufficient *proportion* of the board agrees on the decision;
* whether there are enough board members *taking part* to make the decision valid.

The first point concerns the majority required for a decision to be passed. Sometimes there are special requirements that are set out in an Act of Parliament or in a constitution, but without these a decision is valid if it is passed by a simple majority (over 50%). Note that, unless there is a specific requirement that says otherwise, a simple majority is a majority of those *voting*, meaning that abstentions do not count. For example, if your board has 15 members who are all present at a meeting but only nine of them vote (five vote in favour, four vote against and six abstain), the resolution is passed even though only one-third of the board votes in its favour.

The second point concerns the concept of a quorum, which is the number required to make a meeting valid. A constitution will often set out what the quorum is for a board meeting – in other words, how many of the members need to be present for the meeting to be valid. However, quorums are more frequently specified for general meetings than for board meetings so you may find that your constitution is silent on this matter. Where this is the case, many people's instinct is that this must mean that all board members must be present. However, in fact, the opposite is true. If no quorum is stated, then only two people need to be present for a meeting to be valid. This may seem low, but remember that you should have given notice of the meeting to all of the board members, so everyone has been given an opportunity to be present.

Should it be a requirement of board membership to attend board meetings?

There is no specific legal requirement for board members to attend board meetings, and there will always be some occasions when a board member cannot attend. But regular attendance is not an unreasonable expectation. If a board member is regularly failing to attend meetings, this is likely to raise the question of whether they are truly meeting any of their duties as a board member, such as the duties required by their role as a charity trustee (if the organisation is a charity) or as a company director (if the organisation is a company). The duties of company and charity board members are covered in chapters 5 and 6 (from page 47 onwards and from page 59 onwards) – if you look at these you can see that it is difficult to comply with these duties if a board member does not attend meetings.

Although there is no legal requirement, it is quite common for a constitution to place a requirement on board members to attend meetings. Make sure to check this – your constitution may have a clause that says (for example) that failure to attend three consecutive meetings without the permission of the board means that the person automatically ceases to be a board member.

Other legal requirements

As well as complying with the general common-law principles set out just previously, meetings have to be arranged and held in accordance with a range of legal requirements. These will stem from:

* the requirements of the organisation's constitution;
* any statutes that cover the type of organisation (for example, the Companies Act 2006 for companies).

General meetings

General meetings are meetings of the members of an organisation – not the board. As discussed in chapter 8, there are often times when the members and the board members are exactly the same people. If this is the case in your organisation, it is important to remember that decisions taken by your members *as members* (not board members), such as amendments to the constitution, need to be taken during meetings of members (not board meetings). Such meetings need to be constituted and minuted as general meetings, following all of the necessary legal requirements.

Some organisations are required to hold an annual general meeting (AGM). This makes sense when the members are a different set of people from the board members, or a wider group. This is because an AGM is essentially a means whereby the board can report back to its membership each year. If your membership and board membership are exactly the same group of people, there is really no need to hold an AGM. If this is the situation in your organisation and holding an AGM is a requirement of your constitution, you may want to review your constitution to see whether you can remove this necessity.

Other types of general meeting may be called extraordinary general meetings or special general meetings. These titles are used for any types of general meeting other than an AGM – i.e. for general meetings called for a specific purpose.

A general meeting can usually be called by either the board or a certain proportion of the membership. If your organisation is a company, keep in mind that there is a statutory right, enshrined in the Companies Act 2006, which allows 5% or more of the membership to require a general meeting to be called. If your organisation is not a company, check your constitution to see whether your members have a similar right.

Unless you have a requirement for an AGM, you will only need to call one if you want a decision to be made that can only be agreed by the members and if it would not be appropriate for this decision to be made by written resolution. These types of decision vary depending on the type of organisation and the requirements of the constitution, but they typically include the following:

- **Election of board members:** In many not-for-profit organisations, board members are appointed by the members, and this is often done at a general meeting.
- **Removal of board members:** The requirements for removing board members generally depend on an organisation's constitution. However, the Companies Act 2006 gives the members of a company the right to remove a director (board member) at any time, regardless of what the constitution says. This can be done by a simple ordinary resolution (subject to the required procedures being followed) but it cannot be done by written resolution.
- **Appointment of auditors**.
- **Removal of auditors:** There are a number of provisions in the Companies Act 2006 that refer to the removal of auditors and a number of restrictions on how it is done. It cannot be done by written resolution.

- **Receipt of annual report and accounts:** The board approves the annual report and accounts, but it is usual for these to also be presented to the members. It is a requirement in a company that copies are made available to members, which is often done in a general meeting. The members do not really need to vote on the annual report and accounts, as they are only being asked to receive them (not to approve them), but this matter is often put to a vote.
- **Change of name.**
- **Change of address** (in a registered society).
- **Amendment of the constitution.**

Giving notice of general meetings

As with board meetings, everyone who is entitled to attend a general meeting is entitled to receive reasonable notice of it. However, with general meetings the legal requirements are a lot tighter, both in common law and in the relevant statutes.

First of all, notice does not just have to be reasonable. If your organisation is a company, there is a legal requirement to give 14 clear days' notice (see table 10.1 for a definition) of the meeting. You should also check your constitution to see whether you have a specified notice period and, if so, whether it is longer than 14 days.

A second consideration is the content of the meeting. In the case of board meetings, you need to give members a good idea of the business of a meeting. In the case of general meetings, the requirements are even stricter – you must explicitly state on the agenda every item of business and the exact wording of the resolution(s) that the members are being asked to consider. Therefore, if you are recommending an amendment of the constitution, it is not enough to just say so and allow the details to be determined at the meeting. You must state the sections that you are proposing to amend and the new wording you are proposing. In addition, if a special resolution is to be proposed, the fact that it is a special resolution must be specifically stated.

The reason for these restrictions is that it is vital that everyone who can vote receives full notice of the meeting and can decide in advance whether they want to attend, whether they want to vote and how they want to vote. It is very common to allow proxy voting (see table 10.1 for a definition), and indeed this is a statutory right in companies. Therefore, each member needs to know in advance exactly what resolutions are going to be considered at the meeting so that, if they choose, they can tell their proxy how they wish them to vote. For this reason, items that require a decision cannot be brought up under 'any other business' at a general meeting. It is also generally not possible for a meeting to consider amendments to any of the proposed resolutions (except where an amendment would not change the meaning of a resolution). There must never be a situation where a member can say, 'If I had known that the meeting was going to contain a vote on that issue, I would have come.'

It is possible to hold general meetings with shorter notice periods. The unanimity principle (see table 10.1 for a definition) applies to these types of decisions in the same way as it does to board decisions (but it can only really be used if you have a small membership). In addition, under company law a much shorter notice period can be used if 90% of the members agree. Other types of organisation sometimes have similar provisions written into their constitutions.

The wording of a notice (effectively the agenda) also has quite explicit legal requirements, particular for companies. If your organisation is a company, you will need to inform your members of the meeting's time, place and date; whether there are any special resolutions; the exact wording of each resolution; and members' rights surrounding proxy voting.

Historically, notice of a general meeting was sent out as a hard copy in the post. These days you may be considering communicating with your members electronically instead – it may seem simpler to email people about a meeting or even put the information on your website and tell people it is there, rather than posting the information to them. This is possible as long as you ensure that you are meeting any legal and constitutional requirements – you will need to consider the type of your organisation and what your constitution says.

Many modern model constitutions are worded to enable notice to be given by electronic means (if your organisation is a CIO, its constitution is likely to be worded in this way). However, if your constitution requires hard copies and postage or if there is no wording specifically allowing electronic communications, you cannot use electronic communications without amending your constitution if you are not a company. Company legislation gives companies statutory powers to communicate in this way, without needing to rely on their articles. But you will need to read this legislation carefully. The general rule is that members need to have given consent to receive notice in this way, and often this needs to be explicit consent (usually, you cannot deem the lack of a response to mean consent has been given).

There is a bit more flexibility with regard to the use of a website for electronic communications to members, as consent for communications to be given in this way can be deemed to have been given, but there are quite tight requirements which need to be met. Also bear in mind that when you post a notice on your website, you are still required to notify each member that it is there. Doing so may not be any easier than sending them the notice of the meeting itself.

If you want to communicate and send notices via email or using your website, first ensure that your constitution permits this. If not and if your organisation is a company, look at the regulations regarding electronic communication and the associated guidance to determine whether electronic communication is allowed.

Model AGM notice

Kenttown Civic Centre

Annual General Meeting

NOTICE IS HEREBY GIVEN that the THIRD Annual General Meeting of Kenttown Civic Centre CIC will be held at 6pm on Thursday 25 October 2018, at the Board Room, The Old House, High Street, Kenttown, Kent for the purpose of considering the following business:

1 **Annual report and accounts**
   That the report and accounts for the year ended 31 March 2018 be received.

2 **Appointment of auditors**
   That Audit LLP be appointed auditors of Kenttown Civic Centre CIC until the next general meeting at which the accounts are laid before the shareholders and that the board be authorised to determine their remuneration.

3 **Special resolution: amendment of articles**
   That Article 10.9, which currently reads 'A general meeting shall be convened with 21 clear days' notice', be amended to read 'A general meeting shall be convened with 14 clear days' notice'.

By Order of the Board Secretary

2 October 2018

The Old House, High Street, Kenttown, Kent

A member entitled to attend and vote at the meeting is entitled to appoint a proxy to attend and vote in his/her stead. A proxy form must be received by the Secretary at The Old House, High Street, Kenttown, Kent not less than 48 hours before the time of the meeting.

Outcomes and actions

Meetings are a fundamental part of the operation of an organisation – any board secretary will spend a significant proportion of their time administering meetings. This chapter should have given you an understanding of the different types of meeting that you will need to deal with in the role, as well as the laws and best practice that should be followed. If your organisation has a membership, it could be a good idea to take this opportunity to look back at its past general meetings and consider whether you would organise things differently now that you have read this chapter. Put a plan in place for your next anticipated general meeting (whether annual or extraordinary) so you have a clear idea of what needs to happen when and how members should be notified about the meeting.

11 Resolutions and decision-making

'Resolution' is a term that is used for a formal decision made in an organisation, often following a vote. The term can be used for decisions of either the members or the board, but it is more common for it to refer to decisions of the members. There are various types of resolution.

Types of resolution

Ordinary resolution

An ordinary resolution is one that requires a simple majority to be passed. If taken at a meeting, it is a majority of those present and voting. For decisions taken outside meetings (such as written resolutions), there is sometimes a different majority required.

Special resolution

A special resolution is one that requires a higher majority than usual. Under company law, it is 75% of those present and voting at a meeting. Again, for decisions taken outside meetings, there is sometimes a different majority required. Under company law, certain decisions (such as the amendment of articles) can only be taken with a special resolution. In addition, if a special resolution is proposed in a company, this must be stated in the notice of the meeting and you must use the term 'special resolution'.

If your organisation is a company, another thing to remember about special resolutions is that it was previously a legal requirement for companies that a meeting at which it was planned to consider a special resolution would always require a longer notice period than an annual general meeting. The requirement was 21 clear days rather than 14 clear days. This is no longer a requirement of company law – as a result of the Companies Act 2006 – but it is possible that, if your articles have not been updated since before 2006, this requirement may still remain in place for your company. Also bear in mind that there are still some types of special resolution which require a longer notice period in a company – these concern the removal of directors and auditors.

Organisations which are not companies may have different definitions of a special resolution and may require different majorities – check your constitution if so. It is common outside companies for a special resolution to require a two-thirds majority.

Finally, for unincorporated charities, the Charities Act 2011 requires that decisions to spend endowment funds or to transfer all of the organisation's property require a two-thirds majority.[1]

Written resolution

A written resolution is a decision that is taken in writing rather than at a meeting. This can also mean by email, unless your constitution says something different. For any organisation other than a company, a written resolution taken by a majority of the members or board members is only valid if the constitution allows for it (though bear in mind that the unanimity principle will always still apply; see table 10.1). In a company, a written resolution by board members is only valid if the constitution allows for it. However, the Companies Act 2006 gives a statutory right to members of a company to take decisions by written resolution. According to this statutory right, the majority required is a majority of *all* members, not just those members voting (as it is in a meeting). This means more than 50% of all members for an ordinary resolution and more than 75% for a special resolution.

Additionally, there are two things that the members of a company cannot agree by written resolution: a decision to remove a director (under the rights set out in the Companies Act 2006) and a decision to remove an auditor. Both of these types of decision require a meeting.

For written resolutions covered by the Companies Act 2006, there are further statutory provisions to consider. The company must send or submit a copy of the resolution to every member either by sending copies at the same time or by submitting the same copy to each eligible member in turn. A copy must also be sent to the auditors (if the company has auditors). The resolution must be accompanied by a statement confirming how the member should signify agreement to the resolution and the date by which the resolution must be passed if it is not to lapse. A resolution will lapse if it has not been agreed within 28 days. The date the resolution is passed is the date the required majority is reached.

---

[1] 'Charities Act 2011' [web page], UK Government, 2011, www.legislation.gov.uk/ukpga/2011/25/section/268, Section 268, accessed 13 December 2017.

Example wording: company members' written resolution

Members are asked to consider and agree the following written resolution

Special resolution: change to name

THAT the name of the company be changed from Kenttown Civic Centre CIC to Kenttown Leisure CIC with effect from 1 December 2018.

Members are asked to indicate their agreement by either signing their name below with the words 'I agree' and returning this in the post to the Secretary or, if replying by email, by emailing 'I agree' by return, with this message attached.

The resolution will lapse if not agreed by 28 October 2018.

Example wording: constitution clause on board written resolutions

A resolution in writing agreed by a majority of the members for the time being of the board or by a majority of the members of any board committee who are entitled to vote at its meetings shall be as valid and effectual as if it had been passed at a meeting of the board or of such board committee duly convened, held and constituted.

Getting a quick board decision

You may find yourself in a situation where you need your board to take a decision quickly but there is no meeting scheduled. What are your options?

Convene a meeting

Do not automatically rule out calling a meeting of the board. Provided the constitution gives you the right to do this (as secretary) and you give reasonable notice, you could still have a meeting. Just because your board is not expecting a meeting for some time does not mean that you cannot call one at shorter notice. The advantage of doing this is that it enables the board to give thorough consideration to the item and discuss it fully.

Hold a teleconference

If your constitution allows you to hold a teleconference, this can be a good option. It might be simpler to pull board members together in this way, rather than convene a physical meeting. Remember, though, that this is still a formal board meeting, so reasonable notice still needs to be given.

Teleconference meetings are quite well suited to situations where there is one matter to be considered, rather than a longer agenda.

If your constitution does not allow you to hold meetings in this way, you could use a videoconferencing system such as Skype or you could hold a physical meeting with board members who are unable to attend taking part by teleconference. This would be a valid meeting provided there were enough board members in the room for the meeting to be quorate (see chapter 10 for more on quorums).

Take a decision by written resolution

If your constitution allows, you can take a decision by written resolution. Unless your constitution states otherwise, this can usually be done quickly by emailing all of the board members and asking for their agreement. A written resolution is a good method for a decision that is fairly quick and straightforward and that does not require debate or discussion. Remember to clearly word the resolution on which you are asking the board to vote. There is no point presenting a paper with a loosely worded set of recommendations or course of action and then asking the board to approve this. You need to ensure that there is no ambiguity about the resolution. It is also wise to limit written resolutions to one decision each. If you start to group together a number of resolutions, you run the risk of board members beginning to pick and choose between them, so you have less clarity on who has agreed to what.

Remember that a written resolution by the board is only allowable if your constitution permits it. This is the case even if your organisation is a company. Note that while the Companies Act 2006 appears to give a statutory power to take decisions by written resolution, this statutory power only applies to written resolutions by members.

Use the unanimity principle

Regardless of the decision-making processes that are set out in your constitution or that appear in the relevant statutes, you could rely upon the common-law principle often called the unanimity principle (see table 10.1). This should be the last option that you take, and you should consider it only if no other options are available and the decision absolutely must be taken and cannot be delayed. According to this principle, if all of the board members are in complete agreement, a decision is valid regardless of the way in which it is taken.

To give an example: imagine you have a board of ten members and the general rule is that any decision needs to be agreed by a majority of them.

One day, the chair comes to you and says, 'I was at the pub last night and there were seven board members there. We got to talking about the charity's name and decided to change it. That is a majority, isn't it? So this decision is valid?' The answer is no – it is not. Not all of the board members had the opportunity to take part in the discussion and decision-making. If the decision had been taken at a properly convened meeting, with appropriate notice given, it would have been a valid decision even if only seven had attended and agreed, as all of the board members would have had proper notice. This would have meant that those minority members could have then taken the opportunity to vote, or to try to change the minds of the other board members, or to suggest an alternative that everyone agreed upon. However, if all of the board had been present at the discussion held in the pub and there had been 100% agreement between them all, then this decision would have been valid despite it not having been made at a properly convened meeting. The board members' unanimity would have overridden the fact that there had been no notice, even if they did not call the discussion a meeting.

The unanimity principle also means that you can take decisions by teleconference or written resolution, even if this is not permitted by your constitution, but only if you have complete unanimity of the board.

Note that it is not good practice to rely on this principle, and you are potentially opening up some doubt over the validity of your decision-making if you do. It also requires complete agreement. If your board ever does take a decision in this way, report it to the next meeting and re-confirm the decision at that meeting.

Minutes

Minutes are essentially a record of the proceedings of a meeting and the decisions taken. The board secretary is usually the person responsible for keeping minutes of meetings. While they may not be the person who takes the minutes, they will have responsibility for the minutes. There are certain things to think about when it comes to minutes.

Who should take minutes?

The first thing to think about is whether you are the best person to take the minutes. This question partially depends on your ability to minute accurately but also depends on what other roles you will be undertaking at the meeting. Are you expected to be a participant in the meeting? If so, you really should hand over the minute-taking (you cannot usually do both). If you are a board member and the secretary, you really must ensure that somebody else records the events of the meeting. If you try to do both, you are likely to either not fulfil your duties as a board member (as you will not participate fully) or not minute appropriately. If you have no choice but to minute the meetings, a better way to do it may be to move over to taking minutes by consensus. Take some notes on each agenda item and then, at the end of each item, seek the agreement of the other board members on what you will be recording, in structures such as: 'The key things that we considered in making this decision were..., and [*after discussion*] we agreed...'.

Contents of the minutes

Key features of minutes

- All elements of minutes must be accurate.
- Include some basic information at the beginning – what was the meeting (an AGM for example), its date and who was there. When you record the people who were there, you should separate out the board members from those people in attendance to support the meeting but not to participate in the decisions.
- Minutes must be impartial. Take care if you have been involved in a decision or if you have strong views about it. Minutes must not reflect your subjective view.
- Minutes should reflect the decision made, the key points of any discussion and the reasons why a decision was taken. They may also reflect on the immediate action resulting from a decision, but this is less important.
- Minutes provide an audit trail and evidence that the board members have acted appropriately, so they must be designed to show this. This means that they must show what the board considered when making its decisions, which includes both the papers consulted and the discussion at the meeting. For example, if a board considered an investment and the relevant papers contained advice from a specialist claiming that this was a good investment, this advice should be referred to in the minutes.
- There must be clarity in a set of minutes about the decisions taken, so think about how decisions are recorded. It can be useful to summarise the discussion in the meeting, including any key points that were considered, and then record the decision at the end, in a slightly different way. You could indent the decision, use the word 'resolved' in capital letters or show the decision in bold text.

- Try to avoid listing contributions by name. Sometimes a board member may specifically ask that their view is recorded in the minutes but otherwise it is best practice to avoid doing so. Try to use phrases such as 'in the course of the discussion it was commented that...' rather than something along the lines of 'Mr Minutes said...'.
- In the same way, there is usually no need to record any details of votes. There are examples of constitutions where this is a requirement, but if your constitution does not require it you can just record the decision as taken – resolved or agreed.
- Minutes should be written in the past tense.

Things to avoid

- Minutes are not a record of everything that happened in a meeting or everything that was said.
- Minutes are not a record of how individuals participated in meetings. Most examples of good minutes do not refer to people by name at all – they may summarise comments but they do not usually assign them.
- Minutes can be used as an aide-memoire for the actions to be taken immediately following the meeting, but that is not their primary purpose. Minutes are much more concerned with recording decisions and the reasoning behind the decisions for the long term rather than with setting out the immediate actions following a meeting. You might want to think about preparing a separate action sheet (showing who will do what) that you can circulate very quickly after the meeting.

Example format: recording minutes of a decision

Sale of properties

The Board noted the advice of the Chief Executive to sell two properties to raise money to refurbish the headquarters. There was a short discussion on the timing of these sales and Board members urged the Chief Executive to try to get this matter concluded in this financial year. Independent professional advice had been taken on these sales, and the Board reviewed that report. It was also noted that a full risk analysis had been undertaken.

AGREED: the sale of 18 Dublin Road and 25 Grey Street, at full market value, in accordance with the surveyor's report received.

Outcomes and actions

This chapter has set out the various ways that decisions can be taken and how those decisions are recorded. After reading this chapter, think about reviewing how decisions are taken by your board (and members, if applicable). Consider the following scenarios and questions:

- Think about a time when you have needed a decision to be taken quickly by your board. How did you manage this? Does this chapter give you any alternative ideas?
- Read through your organisation's own board minutes. How do they compare when you consider the key features listed over the previous pages? Are there ways that you could improve the minutes?

There are a wide variety of books and training courses on minute-taking.

12 Regulation

As a voluntary organisation, you are likely to be regulated for a number of reasons. Regulation can be as a result of your legal form, being a charity, the type of work that you carry out or the nature of the services that you provide.

The secretary is not necessarily the person responsible for meeting all of the regulatory requirements of an organisation. However, you will usually be responsible for regulatory matters linked to the legal form of your organisation, and you should have oversight of all of the laws and regulatory requirements that could have an impact on your organisation. There may be other people in your organisation who are responsible for some of the regulatory requirements that your organisation needs to face, but you will still need to know who is responsible for what and ensure that they are clear about this as well.

Sometimes it can seem a bit daunting to try to get a grip on all of the laws and regulations that may have an impact on your organisation. It is therefore probably best to consider everything in sections, starting with your organisation's legal form and how that is regulated, and then moving on to your specific work. This book will not cover and list every single regulation that you may need to consider, but it will give you an idea of some of the things which are most likely to need consideration and will provide ideas regarding ways that you can find out which laws and regulations apply.

The basics of regulation

What is the legal form of your organisation?

It is important to consider the various types of legal form and how exactly they are regulated. If you look back to table 5.1 (page 45), you will see the various types of legal form listed along with the key regulators. You can also see from chapter 5 that the key regulators are Companies House and the Financial Conduct Authority (FCA). In addition to considering those two sources of regulation, this chapter will cover how community interest companies (CICs) are regulated by the CIC Regulator.

Is your organisation a charity?

If your organisation is a charity, you will need to comply with charity law (see chapter 6). The Charity Commission is the regulator of all charities, apart from exempt charities. As well as registered charities, it is also the regulator for small and excepted charities (even though they are not registered with it). Most exempt charities have a principal regulator appointed under the Charities Act to oversee compliance with charity law. If your organisation is a registered charity, there are a number of regulatory requirements that you will need to meet. If your organisation is a charity but is not registered with the Charity Commission, make sure that you understand why not. If it is because you are too small, you will still have a legal requirement to prepare and make available accounts and probably an annual report, but you will not usually need to consider any other regulatory requirements linked with your form. If it is because your organisation is an exempt or excepted charity, this is very likely to mean that you are regulated by a body other than the Charity Commission. For example, academy schools are regulated by the Department for Education and have to meet its regulatory requirements. Registered providers of social housing are regulated by the Regulator of Social Housing and have to meet its regulatory requirements.

Does your organisation provide a service that is regulated?

There are too many different regulators that could apply here, so only a selection are listed. Table 12.1 sets out some of the service regulators that you will need to consider. You will see from this table that the primary areas that are regulated are areas where the service was previously usually provided by central or local government, or now receives funding from central or local government.

Table 12.1   Service regulated areas

Type of service	Regulation?	Regulator(s)
Registered provider of social housing	Yes	Regulator of Social Housing
Health care provider	Potentially	Care Quality Commission; Department of Health & Social Care
Education provider	Potentially	Department for Education

It is unlikely that it will not already be clear to you if you are regulated in this way. It is likely that it will already be clear to you, however, if you are uncertain you can find information about the regulation of your services on the gov.uk website, through any publications that cover your type of organisation, by looking at documents such as your annual report and accounts, or by looking at your constitution. You could also seek the advice of your auditors (if you have audited accounts) or legal advisers.

Does your organisation undertake a function that is regulated?

In addition to the aforementioned service regulation, there are functions that are regulated. Again, there are too many different regulators that could apply here, so only a selection are listed. Table 12.2 sets out some of the function regulators that you may need to think about. In considering which of these may apply, you will need to consult with people in your organisation and get a clear understanding from them of what regulations they think apply to their work. You could also seek advice from any professional advisers and ensure that you are up to date with any applicable regulations, through reading publications of relevance to your work.

Table 12.2 Function regulated areas

Function	Regulator
Personal data	Information Commissioner's Office
Health and safety	Health and Safety Executive
Tax	HMRC
Consumer credit	Financial Conduct Authority
Fundraising	Fundraising Regulator (note, this is a voluntary regulatory system)
Catering	Food Standards Agency
Gambling	Gambling Commission

It is a good idea to set up a list of regulations and regulators that apply to your organisation. This should set out what the regulatory requirements are, who in the organisation is responsible for them, what the timescale is for meeting the requirements, and how your organisation reviews whether it is meeting them. Finally, if a lead is appointed for each set of regulations, you should make it clear that they are responsible for keeping the organisation up to date with any changes.

Charity Commission regulation

There are three types of regulation for those charities that are registered with the Charity Commission:

- information provided to the Charity Commission when an event happens;
- annual updates to the Charity Commission;
- matters where Charity Commission consent is needed.

Information provided to the Charity Commission when an event happens

The Charity Commission holds a register of charities, and this register is available to the public. You can review the register, and your charity's entry on it, at the Charity Commission's website. The details that are held by the Charity Commission on the register are as follows (note that the information shown here in *italic* is held by the Charity Commission but not made publicly available):

- name;
- registered charity number;
- constitution summary details;
- activities of the charity;
- where the charity operates;
- contact details;
- trustees – name, *address*, *email address* and *date of birth*;
- classification – what the charity does, how and with whom;
- financial year (for accounting purposes);
- *main bank or building society details*;
- digital contact details (such as email and website addresses).

Unless the charity is a CIO, there is no legal requirement to inform the Charity Commission of changes to this information when they occur. However, the best practice is to do so anyway and the Charity Commission has an expectation that registered charities will update this information throughout the year.

To access the online register to update the details held on your charity or to file an annual return, you will require your charity registration number and password. If you do not know your password or need a new one, you can request this from the Charity Commission. Note that the Charity

Commission will only send a password to the charity's listed contact address.

In accordance with the Charitable Incorporated Organisations (General) Regulations 2012, the trustees of a CIO must notify the Charity Commission of any changes to information held on the central register within 28 days.[1]

As well as the information set out in the previous bulleted list, the Charity Commission publishes a range of other information on each registered charity, which is collected via its annual return. If a charity submits an annual report and accounts, the past five years' sets of accounts are downloadable from the register entry, along with details of the dates on which they and the annual return were filed. The entry shows details of all charities' income and expenditure going back five years, as well as their current areas of operation.

The Charity Commission states that it is good practice for all charities to report serious incidents to it promptly. Additionally, if your charity's annual income is over £25,000, you must (as part of your annual return) tick a box confirming that all serious incidents during the previous financial year that should have been reported were reported. When you come to do your annual return, if there are any unreported incidents, the Charity Commission advises that these are reported before you file your charity's annual return. It also states that if a charity fails to report a serious incident and it subsequently comes to light, the Charity Commission 'may consider this to be mismanagement, for example, where the trustees have failed to manage the risks properly and breached their legal duties'.[2]

Note that, in many instances, the annual return is completed by an adviser and the box regarding serious incidents can sometimes be ticked automatically, without a full review. For this reason, many trustees do not necessarily know that they are making this declaration each year, but they are. This is one of the reasons why it is important for them to understand their obligations regarding reporting serious incidents.

---

[1] 'The Charitable Incorporated Organisations (General) Regulations 2012' [web page], UK Government, 2012, www.legislation.gov.uk/uksi/2012/3012/schedule/1/made, Schedule 1, Part 3(5), accessed 13 December 2017.

[2] 'How to report a serious incident in your charity' [web page], Charity Commission, 2017, www.gov.uk/guidance/how-to-report-a-serious-incident-in-your-charity, accessed 13 December 2017.

Although it can be delegated, reporting is ultimately the trustees' responsibility. The types of serious matter that should be reported are ones that will or could result in:

- loss of the charity's money or assets;
- damage to the charity's property;
- harm to the charity's work, beneficiaries or reputation.

Examples of serious incidents are fraud and theft, significant financial loss, breaches of legal requirements and any safeguarding issues that arise. When such cases arise, the charity must let the Charity Commission know the details of the serious incident, including how the trustees are dealing with the matter and whether any other regulators or the police have been involved.

Any serious incidents should be reported as soon as possible. The Charity Commission recognises that incidents do occur. If the trustees have handled the matter appropriately, there should be no further action. Further information about reporting incidents is available on the Charity Commission website; the document 'How to report a serious incident in your charity' is particularly useful.[3]

There are some circumstances when the amendment of your constitution will require Charity Commission consent and these are considered in the section on consent (page 120). However, whether or not its consent was required, an updated copy of your constitution should be provided to them. The Charity Commission states that it is a legal requirement for a charity to inform the Charity Commission of any amendments made to its constitution, so that it can keep its register up to date.

You will also need to inform the Charity Commission if you change your charity's name. While you do not need the Charity Commission's consent, it can refuse to register a new name if it is too similar to another charity's name. Always check the register of charities before you decide on a new name.

Annual updates to the Charity Commission

Annual return

An annual return needs to be completed by all registered charities with an annual income of £10,000 or more and all CIOs. If your annual income is

---

[3] See 'How to report a serious incident in your charity' [web page], Charity Commission, 2017, www.gov.uk/guidance/how-to-report-a-serious-incident-in-your-charity, accessed 13 December 2017.

below £10,000, you do not need to complete an annual return, but you will still need to update your charity's details via the the online service the Charity Commission supplies for submitting an annual return.

If your income is £10,000 or more, or if you are a CIO, you must complete an annual return. Currently, the information that you need to provide depends on the size of your charity and the year that you are reporting on. Larger charities, with an income above £500,000, need to provide much more information. The Charity Commission changed the annual return requirements for financial years ending on or after 1 January 2018, and details of the information that must be provided in the annual return are set out on its website. Following this change, for smaller charities, the annual return is still shorter than for larger charities, and most of the required information can be drawn from the accounts. However, to fill it in you will need to know some other bits of key information, such as the number of contracts your organisation holds with central and local government, your income and expenditure outside the UK, and the details of your employees' pay and benefits. The Charity Commission publishes a list of the questions that are asked, and it is a very good idea to study these well in advance of completing your annual return, to ensure that the information is readily available. The Charity Commission's annual return is much more detailed than the confirmation statement that must be filed annually by companies at Companies House.

Charities with an income above £500,001 in the reporting period must complete a much more detailed annual return. This includes a detailed set of questions about the charity's finances, assets and liabilities. Some of the information required to complete this section may be available from the annual report and accounts. Again, it is a very good idea to study the questions well in advance of completing the annual return, to ensure that you have the necessary information.

Note that the Charity Commission does not publish all of the information provided in the annual return; much of it is collected for its own internal purposes. However, a lot of the information published (including summary data on income and expenditure, and the financial history of the charity) is available to access. While you will of course need to provide correct data, you should always bear in mind what data will be published when completing your annual report and accounts and drafting your annual return. For example, are you correctly showing the expenditure on charitable activities, or are you perhaps over-allocating expenditure to governance and administration costs? Remember that the public will be able to see these figures on the Charity Commission's website, and inaccurate information could give an unfair reflection of your charity.

The annual return and the trustees' annual report and accounts (where required) must be completed and submitted within ten months of the end of the charity's financial year. The Charity Commission publishes the compliance history of all charities on the register of charities. Note that this information does not only show the current year – it shows the dates of submission for the five previous years.

All annual returns must be filed electronically. The Charity Commission no longer provides paper forms.

Annual report and accounts

Although only charities with an income greater than £25,000, as well as all CIOs, must send their trustees' annual report and accounts to the Charity Commission, all charities (regardless of their income) must prepare accounts and make them available to the Charity Commission upon request. It is only small, non-CIO charities that can use the exemption.

Those charities that submit an annual report and accounts to the Charity Commission can do so in hard copy or electronically. If submitted electronically, the annual report and accounts must be in PDF format. Note that, if this format is used, the trustees' (and auditors') signatures do not need to appear on the document (provided that a copy has been signed and that you retain this signed copy). In fact, the Charity Commission advises that it is good practice not to submit a signed PDF, to protect the security of the signatures.

The annual report and accounts are usually filed with the Charity Commission alongside the annual return, and they must certainly be filed within ten months of the financial year's end.

Matters where Charity Commission consent is needed

For registered charities, Charity Commission consent is required in the following areas.

Amendment of the constitution

There are some circumstances when the amendment of your constitution will require Charity Commission consent. However, whether or not consent was required, an updated copy of your constitution should be provided to the Charity Commission. The Charity Commission states that it is a legal requirement for a charity to inform it of any constitutional amendments, so that it can keep its register up to date.

This is covered further in chapter 7, but note that for certain types of organisation, and certain amendments to the constitution Charity Commission consent is required in advance of the change being made.

Payments to trustees

A charity will sometimes seek the agreement of the Charity Commission regarding a specific payment to a trustee where it does not feel that the constitution needs to be amended. For example, there may be an occasion when it wants to pay a trustee for a set period of time, for a particular reason, but does not want to give this power ongoing status in the constitution. In such instances, an application can be made to the Charity Commission.

Ex gratia payments

There is no universally upheld legal definition of the term *ex gratia* payment, but it is usually used to refer to payments where the trustees believe that they are under a moral obligation to make the payment but are not under any legal obligation and cannot justify the payment as being in the interests of the charity. It can also include a waiver of rights to money or property to which the charity is legally entitled. These situations most commonly arise when the trustees of charities feel that a payment should be made out of a legacy that the charity has received. *Ex gratia* payments are sometimes permissible, but only with the agreement of the Charity Commission. The Charity Commission issues guidance on *ex gratia* payments and also publishes case studies.[4]

Disposals of land

When a registered charity disposes of land or property, the default position is that the Charity Commission's consent is necessary unless detailed requirements are met. If your charity is considering selling or otherwise disposing of land or property, you should first ensure that you read guidance CC28.[5]

---

[4] 'Ex gratia payments by charities' and 'Ex gratia payments by charities – case studies' [web pages], Charity Commission, 2014, www.gov.uk/government/publications/ex-gratia-payments-by-charities-cc7, accessed 4 June 2018.

[5] 'Sales leases transfers or mortgages: What trustees need to know about disposing of charity land' [web page], UK Government, 2012, www.gov.uk/government/publications/sales-leases-transfers-or-mortgages-what-trustees-need-to-know-about-disposing-of-charity-land-cc28, accessed 23 May 2018.

Use of charitable funds

There is a range of circumstances where there may be specific restrictions on the use of a charity's funds. For example, charity law allows charities to spend funds from a permanent endowment (money or property that is meant to be held by a charity forever) in certain circumstances, but they can only do this with the prior agreement of the Charity Commission. Also, if a charity has a restricted fund (money that can only be used for specific purposes, often because it was donated in order to serve a particular purpose) and seeks to have those restrictions lifted or changed, it needs the approval of the Charity Commission.

Companies House regulation

Many voluntary organisations are incorporated as companies. Such organisations therefore need to comply with a range of regulation requirements that are set out in the Companies Act 2006. The regulator for companies is Companies House, and you can find lots of information on its website (www.gov.uk/government/organisations/companies-house) about the ongoing requirements for companies. However, do note that the information provided is quite general and not specific to not-for-profits or charities. It focuses on filing obligations and relevant time limits.

As with Charity Commission regulation, there is a combination of event-driven filing and annual reporting requirements. The only area where it is necessary to obtain the agreement of Companies House, rather than just notifying it of an event, is in regard to a change of name. However, in this case the new name will be registered provided that it is not too similar to another name and provided that permission has been granted to use any restricted or sensitive words (see 'Choosing your name', page 127).

Note that, if a CIC is converting to a general company (or vice versa), it is necessary to obtain all of the relevant consent from the CIC Regulator. Companies House will need evidence of the required consents before it can make any entries on the register of companies regarding the change.

Event-driven filing

A company needs to notify Companies House as and when the following events occur. Unless stated otherwise, the time limit for notifying Companies House of any of these events is 14 days from their occurrence.

Change of directors and/or secretary and their details

Any changes to the directors or secretary must be notified to Companies House. This refers to the appointment and removal of directors and the secretary but also to any changes to the details that have been filed for them. Hence, if a director's address or occupation changes, Companies House should be notified.

Change of accounting reference date

The accounting reference date is the date the company's financial year ends. For example, if a company prepares its accounts for the period from 1 April to 31 March, then its accounting reference date is 31 March. A company's first accounting reference date is set in relation to the date on which it is incorporated. However, a company can change its accounting reference date, and most will want to do so in order to have a more useful date than that which stems from its incorporation date.

Change of registered office

All companies must have a registered office and this must be a physical place. A PO Box number on its own cannot be a registered office address. A company must always notify Companies House of any change to its registered office. The change only becomes legally effective when Companies House has registered it. Also, a person may validly serve any document on the company at the previously registered address for 14 days after the registration of the form.

Single alternative inspection location

All registers may be held at the registered office address or at a single alternative inspection location (SAIL). Companies House must be notified if a company has set up a SAIL address or if the SAIL address has been moved. A company may only have one SAIL address at a time, so it cannot hold different registers at different locations.

Allotments of shares

If your company is a company limited by shares (such as a trading subsidiary), Companies House must be notified of an allotment of shares within one month of it occurring.

Change of articles

If you amend your articles, you must notify Companies House by sending a copy of the special resolution passed to change the articles, along with a copy of the revisions. This must be done within 15 days of them being passed by the company. Any change to your purposes does not take effect until it has been filed with Companies House. Both the company itself and every officer in default are considered to be committing an offence and could be liable to a civil penalty charge of £200.[6]

Mortgages and charges

A charge (or mortgage) is the security that is given for a loan. Most charges by a company, with very limited exceptions, must be registered at Companies House. You must send details of every mortgage or charge requiring registration to Companies House within 21 days of its creation.

People with significant control

Companies are required to notify Companies House of any people with significant control (see chapter 13, page 138) and of any changes with regard to people with significant control.

Annual filing

All companies, including dormant companies, must submit a confirmation statement at least once each year to Companies House. The purpose of this statement is to confirm that all of the information held by Companies House is correct. If the statement is filed electronically, the fee is £13. You can make the statement at any time during the year, and you can also make it more than once (such as every time you file a change with Companies House). However, you will only be charged once every year.

The information that you need to check and confirm in the confirmation statement is:
- the name of the company;
- the company's registration number;
- the type of company (e.g. private or public);
- the registered office address of the company;
- the address where the company keeps certain company registers (if not at the registered office);
- the principal business activities of the company;
- the name and address of the company secretary (where applicable);
- the names, usual residential addresses, service addresses, dates of birth, nationalities and business occupations of all of the company's

---

[6] 'Companies Act 2006' [web page], UK Government, 2006, https://www.legislation.gov.uk/ukpga/2006/46/section/26, Sections 26(3) and (4) accessed 6 June 2018.

directors (the service address is the official contact address used by the director, where they will receive official government mail – it can be their residential address, but they can choose a different address);
* a statement of whether or not there are people with significant control (if so, who they are and why they have control);
* the date to which the annual return is made up (the 'made-up date');
* (for share companies only) the issued share capital and details of the shareholders.

Annual report and accounts

Companies are also required to file their annual report and accounts with Companies House within nine months of their accounting reference date. Again, this applies to all companies – even dormant companies. Dormant companies and small companies can file accounts in a shorter form, but they must still be filed. If your organisation is a charitable company, the date for filing your annual report and accounts will be one month earlier at Companies House than at the Charity Commission. A company that files its annual report and accounts late will face an automatic late filing penalty. The penalties start at £150 and increase to £1,500 if the accounts are filed more than six months late.

How to file information with Companies House

Companies House provides an electronic filing service (WebFiling) for the vast majority of its event-driven and annual filing; this can be accessed at https://ewf.companieshouse.gov.uk. All of the information previously set out here can be filed with Companies House either online or using a hard-copy form. The annual report and accounts must be filed in hard copy or via appropriate approved and authorised third-party accounting software, although the online system can be used for the filing of audit-exempt accounts and dormant company accounts. Other options for approved software can be found online.[7]

To use WebFiling, you first need to register for a security code, which is personal to you, and then for an authentication code for your company. This is posted to the company's registered office address. Companies House does not send an authentication code to any other address. You will be issued with a different authentication code for each company for which

---

[7] 'Find software for filing company documents' [web page], UK Government, 2018, www.gov.uk/company-filing-software/filing-annual-accounts-returns-and-tax-accounts, accessed 23 May 2018.

you submit information (although you can change these) but just one security code for yourself.

Companies House usually acknowledges and records documents that are submitted electronically very quickly. However, it can sometimes take longer, and electronically filed documents are covered by the same five-day processing targets as paper documents. It is important to remember this and take it into account when filing documents that have a deadline.

Companies House also offers the option of joining its protected online filing (PROOF) scheme. This is designed to protect companies against false filings. If a company signs up to the PROOF scheme, Companies House will not accept forms that can be submitted electronically on paper, unless the company and its directors specifically authorise it to do so by submitting a consent form. This aims to provide added security for companies that file documents because the electronic codes that are used in the PROOF scheme are considered to be more secure than hard-copy signatures. Companies House cannot check the authenticity of signatures on forms, and this can place a company at risk of fraud. If you choose to join the PROOF scheme, you can opt to leave it at any time and return to submitting documents on paper.

Community interest company regulation

There are some additional regulation requirements that apply to CICs. Like all companies, a CIC must submit its annual report and accounts to Companies House. However, alongside these it must also submit an annual CIC report. Additional financial information and disclosures must be included in these reports in order to comply with CIC-specific accounting and reporting requirements. There are two model layouts that can be used for these reports: detailed and simplified, depending on the complexity of the CIC. A CIC with more complex financial arrangements will need to complete a more detailed report. These reports are available to the public via the register of companies.

A CIC that wants to amend its articles needs to complete Form CIC14, which is used to notify the CIC Regulator.[8] This form must include both a community interest statement and a statement of the steps that have been taken to bring the proposed alteration to the notice of people affected by

---

[8] 'Form CIC14: Altering the objects of a community interest company' [web page], Office of the Regulator of Community Interest Companies, 2013, www.gov.uk/ government/publications/form-cic14-altering-the-objects-of-a-community-interest-company, accessed 13 December 2017.

the company's activities. Remember that the prior consent of the CIC Regulator is required for some alterations of the articles, particularly alteration of the objects.

Financial Conduct Authority regulation

Community benefit societies and co-operative societies are regulated by the FCA, to which they must also submit an annual return. The annual return must be submitted within seven months of the society's year end. It is made up of two parts. The first part (AR30) is available from the FCA (www.fca.org.uk/firms/mutual-societies-forms). It is a short form and can be downloaded and completed offline. Once completed, it can be scanned and submitted by email or posted. Part 2 is the annual financial statements (accounts), which must comply with the minimum standards required by the FCA. Failure to submit your return by the due date is an offence which may result in prosecution..

The key event which requires the approval of the FCA is the amendment of the rules. Changes to the rules, including a change of name or a change of registered office, must be filed with the FCA. Such changes do not take effect until they have been registered by the FCA. There are a number of requirements that must be met to ensure compliance with regulations, and the FCA does check through amended rules before approving them. If it considers that there are errors, inconsistencies or failures to comply with law or regulation, the FCA will refer them back to the society.

There are no further event-driven filings for societies regulated by the FCA, other than notifying it of a change to the financial year end and proposals to dissolve or merge with another society. There is an annual fee to be paid . There is no requirement for a society to inform the FCA of any changes to its board members or other information during the year.

Legal requirements: display of name and legal form

One of the major issues regarding administering an organisation that gets neglected is the fact that there are laws and regulations about names. Another concerns the information that organisations must display about themselves.

Choosing your name

Whatever the type of your organisation, there will be restrictions on the name that you can use.

Firstly, if your organisation is incorporated (and there is limited liability), you will need to inform people of this fact – this will usually be done via your name. For this reason, companies and registered societies are required to have a name that ends with the words Limited or Ltd. Not-for-profit companies, as well as registered societies that are charitable or benevolent, can gain permission to omit this word from their name, but if they do so they must show their limited status somewhere on their letterhead. In the same way, a CIO will usually need to have CIO or Charitable Incorporated Organisation at the end of its name. The Charity Commission may agree to register a CIO without one of these terms in its name (e.g. if it would make the name too long), but again the organisation must still indicate that it is a CIO on its letterhead.

Secondly, you cannot use a name that is too similar to another name. If you seek to register a company with a name that is too similar to another company name, Companies House can refuse to register the name. Even if registration is accepted, the existing company can still object to the name. In the same way, the Charity Commission will not register a charity with a name that is too similar to another registered charity's name. There are also laws protecting organisations' brands, identities and trademarks (including trademark law), and injudicious choice of a name carries the potential for legal action to be passed against your charity. This means that you should take care not to use a name that could cause confusion with another entity.

Finally, there are laws on the use of words that are considered to be 'sensitive' (The Company, Limited Liability Partnership and Business Names (Sensitive Words and Expressions) Regulations 2014).[9] While this legislation may seem to relate solely to companies, it now has wider application. Changes arising from the Index of Company Names (Listed Bodies) Order 2017 mean that the register held by Companies House no longer covers companies alone and now includes a wide range of bodies incorporated under other legal frameworks, including registered societies and CIOs.[10] This means that these bodies are now also bound by the aforementioned 2014 regulations. The list of sensitive words is quite diverse, includes geographical terms, and covers many terms that are

[9] 'The Company, Limited Liability Partnership and Business Names (Sensitive Words and Expressions) Regulations 2014' [web page], UK Government, 2014, www.legislation.gov.uk/uksi/2014/3140/contents/made, accessed 20 April 2018.

[10] 'The Index of Company Names (Listed Bodies) Order 2017' [web page], UK Government, 2017, www.legislation.gov.uk/uksi/2017/1233/made, accessed 20 April 2018.

commonly found in the names of charities and not-for-profit organisations. It includes 'charity' and 'charitable', 'foundation', 'institute' and 'society'. These words can still be used in a name, but often you will need to show that the word you want to use is relevant to your organisation and/or show that you have the consent of a relevant body. A full list of sensitive names is published by Companies House, along with information on where to obtain consent.[11]

Choosing a business name

Some organisations use a name in their day-to-day business that is different from their true corporate name (the name on their certificate of incorporation or shown in their constitution). In choosing this name, the key principle is that people need to know who they are doing business with. The legislation requirements in this regard depend on the type of organisation that you are; however, it should be noted that the Companies Act 2006 sets out requirements with regard to business names that cover all types of business and not just companies.[12] If an organisation chooses to use a business name, it must always ensure that its true name is still stated on all business letters, orders for goods or services, invoices, receipts and written demands for payments of debts.

Registered charities

If your organisation is registered with the Charity Commission, you have a legal obligation to say so on the following documents:

- notices, advertisements and other documents issued by or on behalf of the charity which solicit money or property for the charity's benefit;
- bills of exchange, promissory notes, endorsements, cheques, and orders for money or goods purporting to be signed on the charity's behalf;
- bills, invoices, receipts and letters of credit.

It is up to you whether you show your charity number, but doing this is a clear way of evidencing registration. While the list set out above does not cover all of the types of stationery sent out by a charity, it is best practice to always include mention of your charity status on all documents. People in your organisation will use emails to solicit money, order goods and so

---

[11] 'Incorporation and names' [web page], Companies House, 2018, www.gov.uk/government/publications/incorporation-and-names, accessed 4 June 2018.

[12] 'Companies Act 2006' [web page], UK Government, 2006, www.legislation.gov.uk/ukpga/2006/46/part/41, Part 41, accessed 13 December 2017.

on, which means it is best practice for you to have a clear standard signature that includes details of your charity status. It is also a wise idea for your status to be shown on your website.

Company law

If your organisation is a company, you must comply with the requirements of the Companies Act 2006, which are quite extensive. As a company, your organisation must do the following:

- You must clearly show in legible characters the name on the company's certificate of incorporation on:
  - all business letters;
  - all emails and the company's website;
  - all notices and official publications;
  - all bills of exchange, promissory notes, endorsements, cheques, and orders for money or goods;
  - all bills of parcels, invoices, receipts and letters of credit.
- You must show the address of your registered office, your place of registration (England and Wales) and your registered company number on all business letters, order forms and emails, and on your company's website. Even if your registered office address is the only address used on your letterhead, it should be stated that it is the registered office.
- You must show your limited status on all business letters and order forms in legible characters. This is usually done by having Limited or Ltd in your name. However, if you have been granted permission to omit Limited or Ltd from your name (an option for not-for-profit companies), you will need to use additional wording somewhere on your letterhead, such as 'Registered in England and Wales as a company limited by guarantee (company number: 12345678)'.
- You must display the registered name of the company at its registered office, at any place where company records are made available for inspection and at any other location at which the company carries on business (unless the location is primarily used for living accommodation). 'Display' means that the name can be clearly seen by any visitor. If a company is dormant and has been dormant since it was first set up, these requirements do not apply.

Registered societies

If your organisation is a registered society, it must display its registered name at its registered office and at any other location at which it carries on business. It must also display its registered name on all notices, advertisements and other official publications; in all of its business correspondence; in all bills of exchange, promissory notes, endorsements, cheques and orders for money or goods; and on all of its websites.

If your charitable registered society's registered name does not include the words charity or charitable, you must state the fact that the organisation is a charity in legible characters on all of your:

* business correspondence and documentation;
* notices, advertisements and other official publications;
* bills of exchange;
* promissory notes;
* endorsements;
* cheques;
* orders for money or goods;
* websites;
* other documents purporting to be executed by or on behalf of the society.

Outcomes and actions

After reading this chapter, you should understand the regulatory requirements for various types of organisation. You should already have identified your organisation's legal form (see chapter 5) and whether it is a charity (see chapter 6), which means you should now have a better idea of the regulatory requirements that apply to it. You should make a note of which regulators apply to your type of organisation. You could perhaps also take this opportunity to check the websites of those regulators to see how well your organisation currently meets their requirements. It is a good idea to draw up a short plan of what you will need to file each year, when and with which regulator(s). Also make sure that you have a clear record of any codes that you need to use when doing your filings.

This chapter also covers some of the laws and rules on names. Think about how your organisation uses its name, and consider checking your website and email signatures to see whether you are meeting all of the legal requirements that apply.

13 Records and registers

There are a variety of statutory records that an organisation is required to hold. Your organisation will need to keep accounting, VAT (if VAT registered), health and safety, and insurance records. If it has employees, it will be required to keep employment records and records regarding PAYE, national insurance and pensions.

As secretary, you are responsible for the records that relate to the governance of your organisation and to the statutory compliance requirements surrounding the organisation's legal form. The records referred to here are typically called registers, and there are also requirements regarding maintaining minutes as records of meetings and decision-making. The requirements regarding minutes will be covered later, but first you need to know what registers your organisation may need to keep and what form they should take.

For those organisations that are trusts or unincorporated members' associations, there are no statutory requirements. Such organisations may, however, be required by their constitution to keep registers of information, such as a list of members, a list of trustees or records of meetings. If an organisation is a charity, there is also an expectation that minutes will be kept.

Contents of the registers of non-company organisations

Trusts, unincorporated members' associations and chartered bodies have no legal requirements regarding registers, but charitable incorporated organisations (CIOs), companies and registered societies all do.

Trusts

If an organisation is established under a trust deed, it is quite common for no registers to be required by the constitution. Even so, it is still advisable to keep a register of trustees to assist the record-keeping of the organisation.

There is no legal right of access to the registers by the general public unless this is specified in the constitution.

Unincorporated members' associations

As these are organisations based on membership, the most common constitutional requirement is for a register of members to be maintained. The constitution may mirror company law and so may require a register of board members to be kept and sometimes a register of secretaries.

There is no legal right of access to the registers by the members or by the general public unless this is specified in the constitution.

Chartered bodies

These types of body also typically mirror the requirements of company law. Again, as many of them have a membership, the most common constitutional requirement is for a register of members to be maintained. The constitution may also require registers of board members and secretaries to be kept.

There is no legal right of access to the registers by the members or by the general public unless this is specified in the charter.

Charitable incorporated organisations

Every CIO must keep:
- a register of any charges against the property of the CIO;
- a record of appointments of officers made by the charity trustees;
- a record of proceedings at general meetings of the CIO;
- a record of meetings of the charity trustees;
- a record of committees of charity trustees;
- a record of decisions made by the charity trustees otherwise than in meetings.

There are two types of CIO: association CIOs (where the membership is a wider group than the trustees) and foundation CIOs (where the trustees are the only members). In addition to the registers listed above, every association CIO must keep a register of members and a register of charity trustees. Every foundation CIO must keep a register of charity trustees (who are also the members of the CIO).

These registers and records must cover a minimum of the previous six years of appointments, meetings or decisions. The records can be kept in electronic form, but you must be able to reproduce them as a hard copy.

The requirements for CIO registers are set out in The Charitable Incorporated Organisations (General) Regulations 2012.[1]

Companies

The Companies Act 2006 sets out what registers a company must maintain, the information they must hold, how they are to be kept and the public's rights of access. Every company must keep the following registers:

* members;
* directors;
* directors' residential addresses;
* secretaries;
* people who have significant control over the company.

The law requires that the registers are kept at the registered office of the company, at a single alternative inspection location (SAIL) (see chapter 12, page 123) or at Companies House.

The option of keeping the registers at Companies House is a fairly new one for private companies. It is certainly worthwhile to consider it as a way of reducing administrative burden. If a company exercises this option, it is required to keep its information up to date on a public register (at Companies House) instead of on the company register. All of the information currently available for inspection on the company register is then publicly available on the public register. Using this option usually requires the consent of all of those affected:

* If you want the register of members to be held in this way, all of the members need to agree (or, if you are in the process of setting up as a company, you can ask all of the subscribers to agree).
* There also needs to be complete agreement for the register of people with significant control to be held in this way, or this can be agreed at the time of incorporation. After that time, a company can elect to hold the register at Companies House, but it must first give 14 days' notice to the people on the register and it can only go ahead if none of them object in that time.
* A company can elect at any time to have any of the following registers held at Companies House: register of directors, register of directors' residential addresses and register of secretaries. There does not need

---

[1] 'The Charitable Incorporated Organisations (General) Regulations 2012' [web page], UK Government, 2012, www.legislation.gov.uk/uksi/2012/3012/regulation/26/made, Section 26, accessed 6 June 2018.

to be unanimity like there does for registers of members and people with significant control – a majority vote by the board is sufficient.

Registered societies

The Co-operative and Community Benefit Societies Act 2014 requires that all registered societies keep a register of members and a register of officers at their registered office.[2] The term 'officers' refers to the board members, the secretary and office holders (such as a treasurer) if they are not already board members.

The register of members must include:
* name and postal address;
* electronic address (if notified);
* the number of shares held by the member;
* the amount paid or agreed to be considered as paid on the shares;
* a statement of other property in the society held by the member (e.g. loans or deposits);
* the date the person became a member;
* the date the person ceased to be a member.

A registered society must also keep a duplicate members' register at its registered office. This must contain the information in the register with the exception of the information about members' shares and other property in the society, or it must construct the register in such a way that it is possible to open it for inspection without showing this information.

The register of officers must include:
* name and postal address;
* electronic address, if notified;
* the office held;
* the date the person took office;
* and the date the person ceased to hold office.

The registers can be kept as hard copies (in bound books) or in any other way, including electronically. When a register is not kept in a bound book, the society must take adequate precautions to guard against falsification and to make sure that the register is accessible.

---

[2] 'Co-operative and Community Benefit Societies Act 2014' [web page], UK Government, 2014, www.legislation.gov.uk/ukpga/2014/14/contents, accessed 13 December 2017.

Contents of company registers

Register of members

The Companies Act 2006 states that the following information must be held on the register of members:[3]

- the names and addresses of the members;
- the date on which each person was registered as a member;
- the date on which each person ceased to be a member;
- information about the shares a member holds (if the company is a company limited by shares);
- a statement of the class to which each member belongs (if the company has more than one class of member).

It is best practice that the register is maintained for the life of the company. Having said that, entries relating to former members may be removed from the register ten years after the date on which they ceased to be a member.

If the register is not self-indexing and contains more than 50 names, it must be accompanied by an index of the members.

If there is only one member (as is often the case for subsidiary companies), the register of members must contain a statement to this effect.

Register of directors

A company's register of directors must contain the following information:

- name and any former name(s) of the director;
- the date on which each person became a director;
- the date on which each person ceased to be a director;
- a service address;
- the country or state (or part of the UK) in which the director usually resides;
- nationality;
- business occupation (if any);
- date of birth.

If a director is a body corporate or a firm, there are particular requirements as to the details that must appear on the register.

A company must also keep a register of directors' residential addresses. This requirement applies even when the register of directors already

---

[3] 'Companies Act 2006' [web page], UK Government, 2006, www.legislation.gov.uk/ukpga/2006/46/part/8/chapter/2, Part 8, Chapter 2, accessed 13 December 2017.

shows the directors' residential addresses, if they have chosen to use them as their service addresses. However, it can just say for each person that the 'address is the same as is shown on the register of directors'.[4]

Register of secretaries

If the company has a secretary, it should maintain a register of secretaries. This should include:

- name;
- address (a service address can be used and there is no need for a separate register of residential addresses for secretaries);
- the date on which each person was appointed as the secretary;
- the date on which each person ceased to be the secretary.

Register of people with significant control

Companies are now also required to keep a register of people who have significant control (PSC) over them. This register needs to include:

- individuals who directly or indirectly own or control more than 25% of voting rights or shares (for share companies) in the company;
- individuals who directly or indirectly have control over the appointment and removal of the majority of the company's board of directors;
- individuals who otherwise have a significant influence over the company.

The term 'individuals' includes corporate bodies, meaning a company which owns more than 25% of another company would need to be listed. The information that needs to be kept is as follows:

- name;
- date of birth (if applicable);
- nationality;
- country, state or part of the UK where the PSC usually lives;
- service address;
- usual residential address (though this must not be disclosed when you make your register available for inspection or provide copies of it);
- the date each person became a PSC in relation to the company;
- which conditions for being a PSC are met (in other words, what makes them a PSC?).

---

[4] 'Companies Act 2006' [web page], UK Government, 2006, www.legislation.gov.uk/ukpga/2006/46/section/165, Section 165, accessed 13 December 2017.

RECORDS AND REGISTERS ■■■ ··········

This register is therefore needed for wholly owned trading subsidiaries, some companies (where certain parties have rights to appoint board members) and companies with less than four members.

Inspection of the registers

Companies

One thing about company registers that many people are not aware of is that they are public documents; most of the registers of companies are open to inspection by any member of the public. The Companies Act 2006 gives a right of inspection to the public for all of the statutory registers with the exception of the register of directors' residential addresses.

The registers of directors and secretaries must be made available for inspection by any member of the company without charge and by any other person on payment of a fee prescribed by the Secretary of State.

The register of members is also open to inspection. Any member can inspect it free of charge and any other person may inspect it on payment of a prescribed fee. They do not just have a right to inspect – they can also ask for a copy of a company's register of members, or of any part of it.

A person wishing to inspect or obtain copies of a register of members must make a request to the company containing the following information:

- in the case of an individual, their name and address;
- in the case of an organisation, the name and address of an individual responsible for making the request on behalf of the organisation;
- the purpose for which the information is to be used;
- whether the information will be disclosed to any other person.

It is very rare for requests for access to be made, but if you ever get such a request and want to try to avoid giving access to the register your only option is to apply to the courts to ask them to determine that the request is not 'for a proper purpose'. There is no official guidance on the meaning of this term – it is for the courts to determine. However, ICSA: The Governance Institute has a guidance note called 'Register of members access: The proper purpose test'.[5] This is available to its members only,

---

[5] 'Register of members access: The proper purpose test' [web page], ICSA: The Governance Institute, 2017, www.icsa.org.uk/knowledge/resources/access-register-of-members-proper-purpose-test, accessed 13 December 2017.

but it does give an analysis of what may reasonably be considered to be proper or improper purposes, and it may be of assistance to you if you can access it and if you are thinking of challenging a request for access. In any case, your organisation cannot make this decision itself – only the courts can. Furthermore, you must refer the matter to the courts within five days of receiving the request.

If you do not want to comply with the request and instead apply to the court, the court will then consider the request. If the court considers that the request has not been made for a proper purpose, it will direct the company not to comply with it and may award costs against the person who made the request. If the court does not rule in the company's favour, or if the application to the court is discontinued, the company must then immediately comply with the request.

Charitable incorporated organisations

Anyone can inspect or ask for a copy of all or part of the register of trustees kept by a CIO, on payment of a reasonable fee to cover the costs of providing the information. A trustee or member of the CIO can inspect or ask for a copy of all or part of the register of trustees without payment if the request is made either:

- for the purposes of carrying out the requester's duties as a charity trustee or member of a CIO; or
- the requester wants to inspect or see a copy of their entry on the register.

A member or charity trustee of a CIO can inspect or request a copy of all or part of the register of members where:

- the request is for the purpose of carrying out the requester's duties as a member or trustee; or
- the requester wants to inspect or see a copy of their entry on the register.

Registered societies

The right of inspection of the registers is more limited in registered societies than it is in companies. It only applies to the members' register – and, even then, not to all of it. Only the members of a registered society, people with an interest in a registered society's funds and people authorised by the Financial Conduct Authority have a right to inspect the register. This inspection is restricted to their own entry and the duplicate register (or the sections of the register that would normally be contained on a duplicate register).

Keeping minutes

Minutes are discussed in detail in chapter 11, so it might be a good idea to refer back to pages 109 to 111 if you feel you need further information. It is very common for constitutions to require the keeping of minutes of the board, of any general meetings and of any committee meetings. If your organisation is a charity, it is a clear recommendation of the Charity Commission that minutes are kept for the lifetime of the charity.[6]

If your organisation is a company, the Companies Act 2006 has some legal requirements regarding minutes. These are as follows:
- Minutes must be kept of all general meetings for ten years.
- Minutes must be kept of all board meetings and board committee meetings for ten years.
- Records of all written resolutions of the board and members must be kept for ten years.

Despite the ability to dispose of minutes after ten years, it is wise to keep hold of minutes for the life of the organisation.

Minutes are not open to the public in the same way as registers are. However, board members have a common-law right to inspect the board minutes of their organisation. In addition, a member of an organisation has a right to inspect the minutes of its general meetings.

In the interests of being open and transparent, a number of voluntary organisations choose to make their board minutes available to the public – often by publishing them on their website. However, it may be an idea to be aware of the difficulties in doing this. For a board's minutes to fully reflect the decisions of the board and the reasons for those decisions, they need to contain information that a board may not necessarily want to make public. While you may hold some things back as confidential, the likelihood is that you will begin to take minutes with a view to them becoming a public document, rather than whether they fully explain the full consideration given to each item. If your organisation wants to report on the outcomes of its board meetings, it could do this by preparing a report from the board following each meeting. You could use the minutes as the basis for this report, but summarise items differently and hold back

[6] 'Charities and meetings' [web page], Charity Commission, 2012, www.gov.uk/government/publications/charities-and-meetings-cc48/charities-and-meetings, accessed 4 June 2018.

on confidential matters. Reporting in this way also allows you to draw on other information that may help to give more background or context on items.

Minutes are usually agreed at the next meeting of the board or committee and then signed by the chair of that meeting. Minutes that are signed by the chair of the meeting, or the chair of the next meeting, are considered by the courts to be evidence of the proceedings of the meeting. For this reason, it is important that you get a signature, not just an approval. You then need to keep a copy of those signed minutes. You will need to make a decision on whether you keep a hard copy of all of the minutes (in what is usually referred to as a 'minute book') or whether you will keep them in electronic form. If you keep them in electronic form, it must be the signed minutes that you keep – for example, a scanned copy (in PDF form) and not just the Word version of the minutes. You will also need to keep them in a form that you can show is unalterable. For example, if you choose to keep them as PDFs, you will need to lock each PDF so that it cannot be edited.

Keeping the minutes electronically is common practice in many organisations but it is likely to reduce their value as evidence. If your organisation ever needs to rely on minutes as evidence in any legal proceedings, their evidential value could be undermined if there is any doubt as to whether they were signed by the chair or could have been altered in any way. You need to weigh up the risks to the organisation of deciding to hold them in electronic form instead of retaining the original hard copy, and consider this when deciding how best to secure that electronic copy.

Outcomes and actions

This chapter sets out the statutory records that an organisation is required to hold. It also reviews the many types of organisation which are required to keep registers and examines the content of those registers in more detail. You should now have a clear understanding of what registers and records your organisation needs to keep and the form in which they should be kept. Many voluntary organisations fall behind in maintaining their statutory registers in an up-to-date way. If your organisation is a company, you may want to look again at the alternative options for keeping your registers.

14 An effective board

The role of the board

The board of your organisation is responsible for everything, but it cannot do everything. As organisations grow and develop, boards need to move away from functioning on an operational level and begin to take more of an overview. Your board needs to understand its role and focus on the key aspects of its work.

Essentially, the board needs to set a framework for the rest of the organisation to work within, and it needs to then monitor the work that is undertaken on its behalf. It is also the responsibility of the board to fully understand the external environment that the organisation is working within and operate within the law. Board meetings should focus on these roles and the board should keep a check on its agenda items and its discussions to ensure that it is not diverting into operational matters.

You may find it helpful to consider the work of the board under the following headings. When you are planning agendas for meetings, you can identify under which of the headings the agenda item fits. You can also use the headings to begin to check whether the board is fulfilling all of its roles, as well as whether it is allocating too much time and energy to specific areas. An effective board will spend most of its time on setting the strategic framework and monitoring. However, it is important that the other four areas – obeying the law, overseeing the management functions, monitoring and carrying out duties – are covered.

Set strategic framework

Under this heading will come agenda items such as:

- setting the vision, values and strategy;
- agreeing the corporate or strategic plan;
- agreeing the business plan and budget;
- agreeing key policies at a high level;
- reviewing the external environment.

There are likely to be some high-level decisions that will need to come back to the board. Examples of this are approving matters outside the business plan and budget, or approving contracts with significant risks. Generally speaking, one-off decisions like this should be fairly rare.

Obey the law

The board should have a mechanism for reviewing compliance with regulatory requirements and the law. It does not need to do this too often and could delegate the task (to the audit committee for example), but there should be some form of regular review.

Oversee the management functions

This is the heading for the mechanisms that the board puts in place for delegation and internal control. The board needs to be clear about what it is delegating and to whom, and this should be reviewed, perhaps annually. It also needs clarity about what internal controls are in place, and linked with this is the board's work on risk management. Ideally an organisation should have a risk management policy and maintain a register of risks (this is in fact required by some regulators). The board does not need to consider risks at each meeting but it should set the policy, including having a clear idea of what its own risk appetite is. It should also review its risk register (at a strategic level) on a regular basis. It is common for a risk register to be brought to the board twice each year.

Monitor

A board needs to monitor the work undertaken on its behalf, and to do this it requires systems. This includes reports from any committees, regular financial reviews (e.g. the management accounts being brought to each meeting) and performance reviews. It is common practice to develop key performance indicators to be reported back to the board, and some organisations adopt the approach of using a balanced scorecard. There are a number of different monitoring mechanisms available but the board needs to be clear about what information it needs and how this is reported to it.

Carry out duties

The role of the board is linked to the legal duties of the board members. The exact nature of those duties will depend on your organisation's legal type – however, it is interesting to note that there are no very great differences between the legal forms in this area. Essentially, board members' roles and duties are similar across all legal forms. This is because while in some instances the duties are now set out in statute, the essential role of a board member was established in common law.

There are two elements to consider – firstly duties as board members and secondly, if your organisation is a charity, duties as trustees. Refer back to chapter 5 (see page 47) for a list of duties of company directors and refer back to chapter 6 (see page 59) for a list of duties of charity trustees.

Even in an unincorporated, non-charitable organisation, the board members will be responsible for the assets of the organisation, which means they essentially have a fiduciary duty with regard to those assets. If the association has money, the board members, or a small group of them, will hold it in a bank account. These individuals are essentially the trustees of that money and carry the legal responsibilities associated with that status. The courts have always regarded a board member as being a fiduciary – meaning somebody who undertakes to act on behalf of somebody else in a way that creates a relationship of trust.

Board members are also essentially the agents of the members and so they carry the common-law duties of agents. As agents of the organisation, board members have certain duties.

- **A fiduciary duty of loyalty and good faith:** this means that they must act in good faith, in what they believe to be the best interests of the organisation. They should only exercise the powers conferred upon them by the constitution in furtherance of the purposes of the organisation. Finally, they should not place themselves in a position where their personal or business interests conflict with their duties to the organisation.
- **A duty of care and skill:** this duty takes account of any particular skill and knowledge that the board member has, along with the level of diligence that would be displayed by a reasonable person in the circumstances.

These are the basic common-law duties that are conferred on all board members. Beyond that there are a number of legal forms, such as registered societies and chartered bodies, where there is further precedence in the courts that the board members share the common-law duties of company directors. For company directors, these duties are now enshrined in the Companies Act 2006, but this is based on the common-law position and so serves as a good reference point for all of these types of board member.

Effective board meetings

This section concentrates on some of the things that you can do to make your board operate more effectively. It is a key element of good governance that boards work effectively. This section covers three main areas:

- the systems and processes that your board members can put in place to help them to be a better board;
- how the administration of meetings can make the board more effective;
- ways the board can begin to address boardroom behaviour and how this can improve the board's decision-making.

Governance systems and processes

Board performance review

There is now a growing recognition across the voluntary sector that undertaking regular reviews of the board's own performance is a key to good governance. It is now a recommendation in the Charity Governance Code that charities review the board's performance and the performance of individual trustees.[1] The Charity Governance Code recommends that larger charities have an external evaluation every three years – a recommendation mirrored in other codes, such as the National Housing Federation's code.[2] Performance review is now much more widespread across the sector, although for many organisations it is still focused on a collective review of the board's performance as a whole rather than a review of the contribution of individual board members – a board member appraisal.

Organisations often shy away from individual appraisals as they believe appraising a board member who is working on a voluntary basis seems rather negative. However, an alternative way of looking at this process is that it gives each board member the opportunity to sit down each year with the chair (or another board member or an external consultant) and discuss what has and has not gone well for them during the year – in this way, it can be very positive. It gives the board member the opportunity to reflect on their role and raise any concerns that they have. Appraisals of individual board members typically cover things like attendance and contribution at meetings, their views on how the board works together

---

[1] 'Charity Governance Code' [web page], Charity Governance Code, 2017, www. charitygovernancecode.org/en/5-board-effectiveness, Section 5.5, accessed 13 December 2017.

[2] 'Code of governance' [web page], National Housing Federation, 2015, www. housing.org.uk/resource-library/browse/code-of-governance, accessed 13 December 2017.

and their training needs. Even in a small organisation, appraisals do not need to be onerous – they can be conducted quite informally. To undertake their role well, a chair should be ensuring that they meet with each board member individually at least once every year. It typically falls to the chair to carry out such reviews, although the chair may be supported by the secretary or an external consultant may be used. As secretary, it will usually be your job to facilitate these appraisals rather than conduct them.

Performance reviews of the board as a whole vary widely, but they normally address issues such as how effective the meetings are, whether the board receives necessary information and whether there is effective leadership from the chair. Board performance review may be carried out in a number of different ways, and if individual appraisals are being undertaken it is a good idea to run the two alongside each other. For example, if a questionnaire is being used for the performance review, this can be followed up with individual interviews and linked to individuals' appraisals.

Whatever the method of appraisal and review, the process should end with clear conclusions. Board members should receive feedback on their own appraisal and any areas requiring change. Whether the performance review is conducted internally or externally, the conclusions of the collective review, and sometimes a summary of issues arising in individual appraisals, should be put in writing and distributed to the board. This will then serve as a starting point for the board to discuss the next course of action. An implementation plan should be developed to ensure that any proposals are carried through. When the board comes to conduct its next performance review, it should look at the conclusions of the previous review and assess whether or not improvements have been made.

Skills analysis

Another process which is often considered when looking at ways of making boards more effective is a skills analysis. This is a process whereby the board considers which skills, knowledge and experience it deems to be necessary and then identifies any gaps among the current trustees. Can the board fill any gaps by training board members? Can it rely on professional advice for a certain area of knowledge? Should it recruit a new board member with the necessary skills? If you are looking to conduct a skills analysis of your board, there are a number of different methods and templates across the sector. It can certainly be very useful for a board to have a good understanding of its strengths and weaknesses. Be aware of the following if you are undertaking a skills analysis:

- **Subjectivity:** Assessing the skills and experience of board members can be difficult. The usual practice is to ask board members to complete a questionnaire or just to tick against a list. This method does not solve the issue of subjectivity, though. It is important to ensure that you ask the board members to give evidence of their skills and that you have some way of evaluating their responses.
- **Level of skill:** Always think about the level of skill that you require. Does every board member need to have a certain skill? Is it a core competency? Or is it a skill that the board requires, but not from every member?
- **Addressing any gaps:** Do not always assume that you will need to recruit to fill gaps; you may have a board that works very well together despite a gap. You may also find that you have difficulty in recruiting a board member with the skill that you require. Do not forget that, in many instances, once a board is aware that it has a weakness in its areas of knowledge, it can address these through external advice and by seeking more information. Sometimes understanding your skills gaps is just a means of ensuring that you take extra care in your decision-making.
- **Competencies:** It is arguable that what make boards most effective are core competencies. Working together as a team, strategic decision-making and constructive challenges are more important than specific skills. It is a good idea to find some way of measuring these and other core competencies.

Administration of meetings

A fundamental part of your work as secretary will be in setting up and administering the meetings of the board. Much of this can seem mundane, but it does make quite a difference in how effective the meetings are.

The secretary is normally responsible for pulling together the agenda and supporting papers and then distributing these to board members. The information that board members receive prior to a meeting is key to the board's effectiveness, and as secretary you will play a very important part in making sure that board members receive the information in a clear way and in sufficient time, and ensuring that agendas are well structured. In the 'Checklists and examples' section at the end of this book, there is a model format for an agenda with notes on its content (see page 191). Some principles for consideration are as follows:

- Agendas should not be too long (ideally no more than eight substantive items). The board should try to ensure that it retains a focus on the key issues.

- Agendas should be supported wherever possible by papers setting out the matter to be considered and providing background information. These papers also should not be too long. Many organisations provide a standard template for board reports.
- Any recommendations or options in a paper should be clear, and there also needs to be clarity in why the matter has been brought to the board. Is it for information, review or decision?
- Agendas and papers should be circulated in sufficient time. They should be circulated to board members no less than one week before the meeting, so that the members have enough time to read them.
- An agenda's structure should be drafted so that each item is listed, along with its purpose – is a decision necessary, or is the item just for discussion or information?
- Try to guard against the board overusing 'matters arising' and 'any other business'. If a matter arising from the previous meeting needs to be considered, it should be an agenda item in its own right, and 'any other business' should be restricted to urgent or brief matters for information only.
- It is good practice for the board to agree on an annual work programme that sets out what it will consider and when. The secretary is usually responsible for such a work programme, and an example is shown in the 'Checklists and examples' section (see example 5, page 192).

Administration is important. The effectiveness of a meeting can be fundamentally affected by things like the meeting room's setup and location, the length of meeting and the number of breaks in a meeting. Agendas should always have a time limit for each item, even if you (as secretary) and the chair do not share this information with the board (although it is a good idea to do this). When you work out the timings, you should also schedule breaks at fixed times. Board members become less effective and lose attention if they are working on one task for too long. The conventional wisdom on effective meetings is that meetings should not run for more than 90 minutes without a break.

Boardroom behaviour

How board members behave in the boardroom and how they work together as a group is largely in their own hands. Management of this area is a key role of the chair, and as secretary your role is primarily to offer support and advice. But you should have an idea of some of the best practice in this area. As secretary, having oversight of the governance of the organisation and how your board works together as a group is vital.

Having a good chair is essential to ensuring that your board works well as a group. Sometimes, people become the chair because they are quite a dominant force or because they are a very strong spokesperson for the organisation. While these are important characteristics for the external focus of the role, it needs to be remembered that a chair's primary role is to manage the meetings of the board. This means that they need to have a good understanding of the agenda for the meeting, any possible issues and the proposed timing. For each agenda item, they will need to spend their time listening, ensuring board members contribute and then summarising the outcomes.

Board meetings are formal events and need to be conducted in a way that shows mutual respect for the event and all participants. The meeting needs a structure, but it should still be as relaxed as possible and there is no need for an overly formal procedure. Formal votes are not always needed, provided it is obvious that a clear decision has been reached and there is a majority agreement on it. If you are not clear about the decision reached but the meeting has moved on, it is your responsibility as secretary to draw the meeting back to the unresolved issue and check what the outcome was. Often you will just need to do this by saying something like, 'Sorry, but for the minutes can I just check what the decision was on that item?' The chances are that if you are not clear about the decision taken, the board members will not be clear either.

Some organisations find it is helpful to have a written statement of how people should behave in meetings. This can take the form of meeting protocols or a code of conduct. Codes like this usually cover the need to adequately prepare for a meeting, the duty to reflect confidentiality, the principle of collective decision-making, and a prohibition on aggressive and rude behaviour.

Often boards have a view that having a high level of consensus is the sign of a good board, which is not the case. Boards also sometimes develop 'groupthink' – when this occurs, the group is more concerned with maintaining harmony than reaching the best decision. Boards need to become comfortable with the idea of challenge in a meeting. Constructive challenge is a positive force for decision-making and boards need to be careful not to do things to discourage it. This can happen if a board recruits in its own image, encourages only positive contributions or marginalises independent thinkers. Sometimes, when new members join the board who have a more challenging style, this can be seen as having a negative effect on the group. However, it is important to allow challenges to have a place in board meetings.

The final point to consider in how well the board works together is the impact that each board member's personality and behaviour have. A key difference between the two is that behaviour can be changed in a way that personality cannot. When board members have an understanding of each other's personalities, they can begin to be aware of how this influences their decision-making. In turn, they can start to change their behaviour as a group to accommodate it.

Outcomes and actions

This chapter should have given you a number of ideas on how to make your board more effective. An effective board is key to having a well-governed and well-managed organisation. As board secretary you should play a central role in aiding that effectiveness. However, you will also need to get the board onside when making any changes. This chapter should have given you some ideas about your next steps. Consider sharing some of these behind-the-scenes insights with your board members as one of your first steps.

15 Good governance

What is good governance?

Governance as a term has a number of definitions, but it is effectively about the processes and framework for the decisions of an organisation, rather than the decisions themselves. Boards of directors are responsible for the governance of their companies. Shareholders' role in governance is to appoint the directors and the auditors and to satisfy themselves that an appropriate governance structure is in place. The responsibilities of the board include setting the company's strategic aims, providing the leadership to put them into effect, supervising the management of the business and reporting to shareholders on their stewardship.

There is a key difference between governance and management. Governance is about the work of the board – meaning its leadership, strategic decision-making, oversight and accountability. Management is about operational matters and the day-to-day management of the organisation. This is delegated by the board and often undertaken by staff. It should be done within the strategic framework that is set by the board. Management is effectively about the implementation of the strategy set by the board.

The larger the organisation, the easier it is to see a distinction between governance and management. If your organisation is a small one, perhaps with no staff, it may seem disingenuous to try to divide out governance and management. Perhaps in your organisation the board does both. While this may be true in some smaller organisations, it is still necessary to separate out the two functions as they go hand in hand. Governance processes should enable you to conduct management in a more effective way.

As an example, a key element of good governance is effective board working, with meetings being focused on the key roles of the board and being outcome-based. Your board may be taking management decisions at the board meeting, but ensuring that those meetings are run effectively will make that decision-making better. You also want to ensure that those decisions are taken within a strategic context – this way, the board will not be firefighting all the time, and each decision will build on and fit together with another. Again, this is about making sure that the governance of the organisation enables its management to be more effective. Without this framework, you may find that your board ends up making duplicate or conflicting decisions. It might even constantly reverse previous decisions and not stick to its core purpose.

Governance is important even if your board still needs to make management decisions. Then, as your organisation grows, you will need to use your good governance systems to move the board away from operational matters, clearly delegating these matters and monitoring the board's progress. The board can then free itself to focus on strategic direction. Governance is ultimately about effective decision-making.

Why does governance matter?

A question often arises regarding whether all of these frameworks, processes and efforts surrounding behaviour really make a difference to an organisation. It may all sometimes seem a bit unnecessary. It is certainly true that you need to ensure that any framework and processes that you put into place are proportionate to your organisation. However, many people see governance as no more than a matter of bureaucratic red tape – things that you have to do and boxes that you have to tick to satisfy regulators.

There are undoubtedly some organisations out there that have a board only because they have to. The organisation may have adopted a legal form that requires a board (it is hard to find a legal form that does not) because it was expected to do so. But the board may not be the real decision-making body – it may do no more than rubber-stamp decisions. It may even be the case that it rarely meets (there was one case investigated by the Charity Commission in recent years where the board had never met). It may be the founder or the chief executive who is really running the organisation.

Other organisations may have quite detailed governance structures, with committees meeting regularly. But those committees may not have any real delegated powers, and the board may duplicate most of their work. It is also possible to find organisations that have adopted detailed standing orders, schemes of delegation, role descriptions and codes of conduct but have then effectively locked them away in a drawer. On paper these organisations look very well governed, but the reality is that nobody is paying any regard to the official processes and structures.

Perhaps the key thing about these examples is not just that they are quite widespread but that many of these organisations may seem to be functioning perfectly fine. We have to be honest and admit that even some pretty effective organisations are being governed poorly. But it is when you look at it the other way around that the importance of good governance becomes particularly apparent: it is hard to think of any ineffective organisations that are governed well. Does a poorly governed organisation just need luck to do well? Not really, but it is also a question of timing. A poorly governed organisation can be effective for a period, but not indefinitely. In time, the weaknesses of its poor governance will catch up with it as it tries to grow, change, adapt or face challenges.

Governance failures

Another way of looking at the importance of governance is to review examples of where it has gone wrong. The reality of the voluntary sector is that there are few well-known examples of organisations failing, through poor governance or otherwise. This is a sector made up of a vast array of small organisations, many of which will quietly and discreetly fail and fold. However, a few examples can be found by looking towards some of the rare big failures, which can be very revealing.

Three examples of governance failures that are of relevance to the voluntary sector, and that are worthwhile reviewing, were in Kids Company, Cosmopolitan Housing Group and the Co-operative Bank. Reports on these organisations are included in the further reading list at the end of the book (see page 203). You may wonder at the inclusion of the Co-operative Bank as an example, as it is clearly not a voluntary organisation. However, much of its ethos and ways of operating were shared with the sector. It is useful to look at the Co-operative Bank because of its method of appointing board members and the implications that this seemed to have for its governance.

It can also be helpful to look at the Charity Commission's review of charities (its cases include statutory inquiries, operational compliance cases, monitoring cases and whistleblowing cases, but the generic term 'investigations' can be used). The Charity Commission now conducts quite a few investigations into charities each year (in 2017 it opened 1,664 new compliance cases) and publishes reports on each one of these investigations; it also issues an annual report on these matters – the latest report covers 2016 to 2017.[1] This report highlights that poor

---

[1] 'Tackling Abuse and Mismanagement 2016–17: Full report' [web page], Charity Commission, 2018, www.gov.uk/government/publications/tackling-abuse-and-mismanagement-2016-17/tackling-abuse-and-mismanagement-2016-17-full-report, accessed 27 March 2018.

governance is a factor in many of the cases that reach the Charity Commission. It states that governance issues came up in 618 of its new regulatory compliance cases and in 484 of the closed cases. It also states that 65% of the whistleblowing cases that it dealt with were related to governance issues. The primary governance issues that it came across were:

- conflicts of interest;
- private benefit;
- decision-making and recording decisions;
- individuals applying significant control or influence.

In my experience, it seems that the four key areas of governance failure that are most commonly identified across the sector are:

- dominance (linked with individuals applying significant control or influence);
- conflicts of interest;
- delegation (linked with decision-making);
- issues surrounding information and understanding (also linked with decision-making).

Clearly, good governance is important and it does influence the effectiveness of an organisation. You may have a board which is tired of hearing the word governance and will never see it as relevant. In this case, why use the word governance? What you are really talking about is making the board more effective, and this should be music to the ears of your board members.

A changing approach to governance

Another thing to note is that, historically, good governance was very much about having what were perceived to be best-practice procedures and frameworks in place, but this focus has changed. This approach to governance was in fact quite prescriptive, and good governance was often perceived to be concerned with having quite a lot of governance-related paperwork in place (terms of reference, codes of conduct, role profiles, etc.) and quite a lot of meetings (e.g. of committees). Often these were frameworks and processes designed for large organisations and then applied to smaller ones, and they did not necessarily fit. As a result, there began to be a shift in thinking towards the idea that governance needed to be more proportionate to the organisation.

At the same time, the financial crisis of 2008–2009 led to a rethink of governance. There were significant failures in a number of banks that were the result of poor decision-making by their boards. These were organisations that should have been well managed – the banking sector did in fact have quite a lot of governance regulation. So why did things go wrong? In 2009, ICSA: The Governance Institute published a report (the Walker Report) that developed the concept of behavioural governance.[2] This report addressed the issue of why governance failures had occurred in these companies. The report concluded that the effectiveness of the governance systems had been undermined by a failure to observe appropriate boardroom behaviour. It stated that appropriate boardroom behaviour was an essential component of good corporate governance and went on to identify some of the characteristics of good boardroom behaviour. These included:

- a clear understanding of the role of the board;
- the appropriate use of knowledge, skills, experience and judgement;
- independent thinking;
- the questioning of assumptions;
- constructive challenges.

Since 2009 there has of course been some change in how governance is reviewed. It is no longer just about the systems and processes and now also covers how board members behave. In recent years, those who look at how good an organisation's governance is have come to include consideration of how well the board works together as a team, whether there are effective challenges and independent thinking, and the personality types of the individual board members. Governance reviews are much more focused on the overall effectiveness of a board and its decision-making. Linked to this is a key recognition of the fact that meetings need to be effective and board members need to clearly understand their roles.

Governance codes

Overview of the use of codes

The history of the growth of governance within the UK has been fundamentally linked with the use of governance codes. In the UK, governance requirements are not founded in the law. There are some applicable laws, depending on the type of organisation. These cover matters such as the legal responsibilities of your board members, and they

---

[2] *Boardroom Behaviours: A report prepared for Sir David Walker by the Institute of Chartered Secretaries and Administrators ('ICSA')* [PDF], ICSA: The Governance Institute, 2009, www.icsa.org.uk/assets/files/pdfs/consultations/09.04%20ICSA%20Policy%20Report%206.pdf, accessed 13 December 2017.

provide some criteria for who is eligible to serve on a board. There are also laws relating to reporting and record-keeping, which relate to the governance area of accountability. Beyond that, it is really for an organisation to determine its own standards of governance. That said, a number of regulators and funders will have expectations regarding how well your organisation is governed. These expected standards are often set out via a governance code. Organisations can be expected to adopt and follow a code, and report on any areas of non-compliance.

Organisations began to consider their governance processes after the work of the Cadbury Committee. This committee was set up in May 1991 by the Financial Reporting Council and the Stock Exchange to look into growing concerns about standards of corporate governance, financial reporting and accountability. The first real governance code (which used to be called the Combined Code) developed out of the work of the Cadbury Committee. From this point, how organisations were governed was no longer just a private matter for them to consider internally; it became a point of public record. If an organisation wanted the support of the public – whether through increasing the price of its shares, achieving a listing on the stock market (for a commercial organisation), or receiving donations or funding (for a voluntary organisation) – it now had to behave according to certain expectations.

If you are reviewing the effectiveness of your governance, a code is a very good place to start. You may have a regulator that expects you to follow a certain code, or you may be able to choose which one is more applicable to your organisation – either way, looking at a code and considering how you measure up against it, and what you need to do to comply with it, is a very good way to begin to review your own governance. It gives you a framework for that review, ensures that you cover all aspects of governance and gives you an understanding of the best practice for organisations that are similar to yours.

The next section of this chapter lists some of the main codes that you may wish to consider. These are short summaries, showing the types of organisation that they apply to, notes on their content and format, and a bit of the background to each particular code. Details of each of the organisations or bodies that publish a code are included in the useful addresses section at the end of this book (see pages 197–202), and an up-to-date copy of each code will usually be available from the relevant organisation's website. In most cases these codes are free to download and use, but in some instances a small fee is payable.

Registered providers of social housing are regulated by the Regulator of Social Housing and need to meet its regulatory standards, including its

Governance and Financial Viability Standard.[3] The most recent version of this was published in April 2015 and it is a requirement of this standard that registered providers adopt and comply with an appropriate code of governance. Registered providers must report on any areas of non-compliance in their annual report each year. While organisations have flexibility as to which code they can adopt, it needs to be an established code. A registered provider cannot create its own code.

Another example of organisations that are required to use a code are sporting bodies that seek to receive public funding. In 2017, UK Sport and Sport England launched a collaboratively developed code called the Code for Sports Governance. This sets out the standards expected of organisations that seek funding from the UK government or lottery funding. A sporting body needs to show commitment to the code in order to receive public funding.[4]

UK Corporate Governance Code

The UK Corporate Governance Code is one of the longest-standing codes worldwide and was previously called the Combined Code. It is the code that is applicable to companies that are listed on the London Stock Exchange. It is therefore designed for large commercial companies. It is a requirement of listing on the London Stock Exchange that companies 'comply or explain'. This means that, while it is not a requirement for a company to comply with the code, it is an expectation. The company is required to set out in its annual report how it has complied and any areas of non-compliance, along with the reasons for this.

Private, unlisted companies do not need to consider the code or make any statement in their annual reports in regard to it, but it is suggested that it is good practice for them to take it into account. The code is principle-based (as opposed to prescriptive).

This code is not usually of relevance for voluntary organisations, but it is useful to have some understanding of it, as it contains many of the principles and recommendations that over time have become accepted indicators of good governance across all sectors. Examples include:

---

[3] *Governance and Financial Viability Standard* [PDF], Homes & Communities Agency, 2015, www.gov.uk/government/uploads/system/uploads/attachment_data/file/419368/Governance_and_Financial_Viability_Standard_2015.pdf, accessed 20 September 2017.

[4] *A Code for Sports Governance* [PDF], Sport England/UK Sport, 2016, www.sportengland.org/media/11193/a_code_for_sports_governance.pdf, accessed 13 December 2017.

- the importance of an audit committee;
- the approach to risk;
- the importance of independence on the board.

Some voluntary organisations which are quite commercial in their focus and work with third parties that have an understanding of this code (and expectations relating to it) might find it a good code to follow. Some registered providers of social housing adopt this as their code. However, it needs to be remembered that this code is designed for a very different type of organisation and key sections of it will not be applicable. For example, there is much in the code that is concerned with the remuneration of the board and consequently with the need for a remuneration committee. This will not be relevant for a voluntary organisation that has an unpaid board. The code also has expectations of governance that may be out of proportion for a smaller organisation – for example, many voluntary organisations will be too small to need (or justify having) an audit committee.[5]

Charity Governance Code

The Charity Governance Code is the code that is most commonly used in the voluntary sector and it was last reviewed in 2017. It was previously called the Code of Good Governance for the Voluntary and Community Sectors and, although its focus has shifted to charities, it was originally designed for all types of voluntary organisation.

The code was first developed in 2005 and has gone through a number of changes. There have essentially been three main stages in its development. It first began life as quite a detailed, prescriptive code that seemed to have been based upon the Combined Code. It was used by many voluntary organisations, particularly charities, and was seen as a real step forward in the development of voluntary sector governance. However, because it was so detailed, it was really only suitable for larger organisations that already had quite an extensive governance structure in place. Over time, a version of the code was developed for smaller organisations, but this was not so widely used. Following the development of the concept of behavioural governance, there was a move across all sectors away from codes being too prescriptive, and many codes become much more principle-based. This happened with the UK Corporate

---

[5] *The UK Corporate Governance Code* [PDF], Financial Reporting Council, 2016, www.frc.org.uk/getattachment/ca7e94c4-b9a9-49e2-a824-ad76a322873c/UK-Corporate-Governance-Code-April-2016.pdf, accessed 13 December 2017.

Governance Code and it also happened with the Code of Good Governance, which was re-launched in 2010 as a principle-based code. It was simpler to follow and suitable for a wider range of organisations. However, it was sometimes perceived as too sweeping in its format and not clearly focused enough on the requirements of good governance. The code underwent revisions in 2015 and 2016, with wide consultation in 2016, and was finally re-launched as the Charity Governance Code in summer 2017. The revised code is now explicitly designed for charities and outlines much higher standards to which all charities are expected to aspire.

The code is fully endorsed by the Charity Commission, which has decided to withdraw its publication *Hallmarks of an Effective Charity* and instead refer charities to the code. Charity Commission guidance issued since the publication of the code has indicated that it now has an expectation that charities will take the code into account and follow it:

> The Charity Governance Code represents a standard of good governance practice to which all charities should aspire. We encourage all charities to read, follow and apply it proportionately to their circumstances.[6]

The Charity Governance Code offers one code for all charities regardless of size. There are sets of principles and outcomes that apply to all charities and then two sets of recommendations – one for smaller charities and another for larger charities. It is also suggested that charities that adopt the code begin to work under the principle of 'apply or explain', which means setting out in their annual reports that they have indeed adopted the code and then going on to explain any areas where it has not been applied.

The drafters of the code were clear that they wanted it to set high targets for charities to seek to work towards, rather than minimum standards to be followed. In this way, the code returned to a form that is more prescriptive and more demanding than the previous principle-based approach.

Some of the key features of the code are:
- an expectation that the board will publish its register of interests;
- a strong expectation that charities will review individual trustees' performance and the board's performance (there is a recommendation that larger charities have an external evaluation every three years);
- a recommended maximum term of office for trustees of nine years;
- links between the code and the duties of charity trustees;

---

[6] Sarah Atkinson, 'The New Charity Governance Code – Essential reading for all trustees' [web article], Charity Commission, 2017, https://charitycommission.blog.gov.uk/2017/07/13/the-new-charity-governance-code-essential-reading-for-all-trustees, 13 July 2017.

- consideration of the impact of boardroom behaviour (for the first time in the history of the Charity Governance Code and Code of Good Governance).

The code is available online.[7]

Co-operative codes

The organisation Co-operatives UK has developed three model codes that are suitable for co-operatives and can be used and adapted by them. These are entirely voluntary codes – there is no requirement for a co-operative to operate within them. The three codes are:

- Corporate Governance Code for Consumer Co-operatives;
- Worker Co-operative Code;
- Corporate Governance Code for Agricultural Co-operatives.

These can be found online.[8]

Code for Sports Governance

As set out earlier, the Code for Sports Governance must be used by sporting bodies that seek to receive public funding. It sets out the standards expected for organisations that seek funding from the UK government or lottery funding. If a sports body cannot show its commitment to the code, it will not receive public funding.

The code can be found online.[9]

National Housing Federation Code of Governance

The National Housing Federation Code of Governance is a model code designed for registered providers of social housing. As set out previously, providers that are registered with the Regulator of Social Housing must adopt a relevant code and report on their compliance with it. A registered provider can choose which code to follow and it does not need to adopt the National Housing Federation Code, but the reality is that most registered providers do. The code is therefore seen as best practice for the governance of registered providers.

---

[7] 'Charity Governance Code' [web page], Charity Governance Code, 2018, www.charitygovernancecode.org, accessed 24 May 2018.

[8] 'Codes of governance' [web page], Co-operatives UK, 2018, www.uk.coop/developing-co-ops/grow-your-co-op/codes-governance, accessed 24 May 2018.

[9] 'A Code for Sports Governance' [web page], UK Sport, 2017, www.uksport.gov.uk/resources/governance-code, accessed 24 May 2018.

This is quite a detailed and prescriptive code. It sets out requirements for a maximum term of office of nine years for board members, requires an audit committee (which the chair must not be a voting member of) and requires all board members to be recruited and appointed on the basis of a skills analysis. The code was last reviewed in 2015. Although it is designed for registered providers, there is nothing to stop other forms of organisation using the code. A fee is payable to the National Housing Federation for use of the code.

The code can be downloaded from the National Housing Federation's website.[10]

Academy schools governance codes

There is no model code for academy schools or multi-academy organisations, but there are a number of applicable guides that have been developed by the Department for Education for governing bodies in local-authority-maintained schools and boards of trustees in academies. These include a governance handbook that covers the governing boards' role, the associated legal duties and the main features of effective governance. There is also guidance entitled 'A competency framework for governance' that is designed to set out the knowledge, skills and behaviours that an academy governing board needs to be effective. These are both available from the Department for Education and can be accessed online.[11]

NHS Foundation Trust Code of Governance

There is a governance code for NHS foundation trusts. This is published by Monitor and was last updated in July 2014. It is designed especially for foundation trusts, but it may be a useful code to review if your organisation provides health services or works closely with the NHS. It can be accessed online.[12]

[10] *Code of Governance: Promoting excellence for housing associations* [PDF], National Housing Federation, 2015, http://s3-eu-west-1.amazonaws.com/pub.housing.org.uk/CodeGov2015-FINAL.pdf, accessed 24 May 2018.

[11] 'Governance handbook and competency framework' [web page], Department for Education, 2017, www.gov.uk/government/publications/governance-handbook, accessed 24 May 2018.

[12] 'NHS foundation trusts: Code of governance' [web page], Monitor, 2014, www.gov.uk/government/publications/nhs-foundation-trusts-code-of-governance, accessed 24 May 2018.

International Framework: Good Governance in the Public Sector

International Framework: Good Governance in the Public Sector is a governance code designed for the public sector. It was prepared by the International Federation of Accountants and the Chartered Institute of Public Finance and Accountancy. The latest version was published in July 2014. While it is intended to establish a benchmark for good governance in the public sector, it may be of interest and use to voluntary organisations that provide public services. The code can be accessed online.[13]

Governance frameworks

The constitution of your organisation will set out how your board is appointed and it may also specify a term of office for board members. In a small organisation, the governance framework may comprise the board and nothing more, or you may just have a board and a team of staff to whom the board delegates.

Other organisations may have committees. A board with committees reporting to it is the most common type of governance framework.

It might help to have a document that sets out the governance framework of your organisation. This can be useful in ensuring clarity and avoiding gaps and inconsistencies. Often these types of document are called 'standing orders', but you do not need to use this title and it can seem rather unclear to those unfamiliar with governance. You could call it 'governance procedures' or 'governance framework'. The document will usually contain the following information:

- the role of the board and the matters reserved by the board;
- any additional information (other than that set out in the constitution) on the composition and size of the board;
- the systems to be followed for board meetings and board decisions (what notice will be given for meetings, when minutes are normally prepared and how decisions are taken, such as by written resolution);
- the principles of delegation (often a scheme of delegation is included as an appendix);
- committees of the board (including their terms of reference);
- financial regulations;

---

[13] 'International Framework: Good Governance in the Public Sector' [web page], Chartered Institute of Public Finance and Accountancy, 2014, www.cipfa.org/policy-and-guidance/standards/international-framework-good-governance-in-the-public-sector, accessed 24 May 2018.

- the role of the auditors (internal and/or external), if the organisation has them;
- how conflicts of interest are handled;
- risk management procedures.

Board size and composition

The boards of voluntary organisations are becoming smaller in their average size, as identified by the Compass Partnership.[14] This may be as a result of the difficulties many organisations face in recruiting board members, but it is also because there is a growing understanding of the need for a board to work well together – and smaller groups work better. There is also more recognition in the sector of the legal duties of board members and so it is becoming less common to have people appointed to boards who do not take an active part in them. The average board size in the organisations surveyed by the Compass Partnership was 14, but 27% of the organisations had boards with fewer than ten members. Also, this was a survey of large charities – small organisations tend to have smaller boards.

There is no definitive view on the optimal size of a board – it depends on the organisation, and it is true that voluntary boards tend to be larger than commercial boards. However, if you are reviewing the constitution and governance of an older organisation, you may find that you have a requirement for a board that is bigger than what is really necessary. Board members should be regularly attending and contributing to meetings. Often with larger boards, you may find that you have a lower level of attendance and some board members may not be contributing much to meetings. Consider whether your board is perhaps larger than it needs to be.

Remember as well that a board can be too small. If your organisation is a registered charity, you should note that the Charity Commission recommends that a board should not have fewer than three members. Having a very small board is sometimes essential when an organisation is just beginning to operate, but after the initial period it can be an indication of a person taking a dominant role in running the organisation. It can also mean there are likely to be insufficient skills represented on the board.

---

[14] Mike Hudson and Jacinta Ashworth, *Delivering Effective Governance: Insights from the boards of larger charities*, London, Compass Partnership/Centre for Charity Effectiveness/Cass Business School, 2012.

Another thing to consider regarding board composition is the term of office for board members. It is best practice for a board member to be appointed for a fixed term (which may be renewable) and not an indefinite period, and for there to be a maximum term of office for board members. When board members serve for a very long period of time (without regular review), there can be a real risk of complacency and of the board becoming stale. There will always be exceptions, and there will be some instances when a long-standing board member is still adding to the effectiveness of the organisation or where there is no option to bring on new board members. Nonetheless, encourage your board to set terms of office and maximum terms, and to do what it can to draw in new trustees.

In many organisations, the constitution will provide that it is up to the board to recruit and appoint new board members. However, some organisations with a large membership may have an elected board and some may give other bodies the right to nominate onto the board.

It is best practice across the sector for recruitment to be open and transparent, and boards should be recruiting on the basis of a skills analysis (see chapter 14, page 147). Having elected or nominated board members does not need to prevent this happening. With an elected board, the board itself can still identify skills gaps and encourage candidates with these skills to stand for election. It can also ensure that the voters know what skills they should be considering when voting. Often a constitution will also then allow for additional board members to be appointed to fill any skills gaps after these elections. Where board members are nominated, the nominating body can also be advised of the skills gaps on the board and asked to consider this in making its nominations.

It also needs to be remembered that nominated and elected board members cannot act on behalf of the nominating body or the people who elected them (see chapter 5, page 47, for more on the duties of board members of a company, and chapter 6 page 59 for board members of a charity).

Committee structure

A board may choose to establish committees to work on its behalf. When it does so, it needs to agree clear terms of reference for each committee. These should set out the following points:

* who the members of the committee will be and how they are appointed (usually by the board);
* how the committee will be chaired;
* how often the committee will meet;

- the functions of the committee – what it does;
- the powers of the committee – whether it is advisory only or has any delegated powers;
- how the committee will report back to the board.

A model format for terms of reference is set out at the end of this section.

Committees can be a useful way to consider matters in more detail and they can devote time to a matter in a way that the board generally cannot. Also, their membership does not need to be restricted to board members, so this can be a useful way of drawing in additional expertise. However, the board should be clear about each committee's purpose. There are matters that a board should never delegate, and it should also ensure that a committee does not end up duplicating some of the board's work. It can sometimes happen that a matter is delegated to a committee and then considered by the committee in detail, but the committee then reports back to the board and the board considers the matter in full all over again.

In addition, if your board is giving committees delegated powers and your organisation has a staff, you will need to guard against duplicating that delegation. Committees can be a useful way of monitoring on behalf of the board and scrutinising the work of staff on a more detailed level. In small organisations that lack staffing resources, it can be helpful if committees are asked to authorise operational decisions, but in other organisations this can create a lack of clarity about who does what. Whenever committees are asked to authorise strategic decisions, it is important to check whether the board is properly fulfilling its role.

The types of committee that you have will depend on the needs of your organisation. Note that the need for a particular committee may be set out in your constitution. The most common type of committee across the sector is the audit committee. Some organisations also follow the model set out by the UK Corporate Governance Code and have nomination committees and remuneration committees (usually concerned with staff remuneration instead of board remuneration, as board members tend to be unpaid).

As well as committees, it is quite common within the sector for an organisation to have some form of assembly, advisory council or other similar body. Sometimes this group appoints to the board and sometimes it is purely advisory. The typical role for such a group is to be consulted on strategy and direction and to provide non-binding strategic advice to the board, so this can be a very useful way of seeking the views of key stakeholders or beneficiaries. However, care needs to be taken to ensure that there is real clarity about the role and that there is no confusion about the fact that it is the duty of the board members to set the strategy and direction, and not the advisory council, even if they have been consulted upon it.

Model: terms of reference
[insert committee name] Committee

1. Purpose

The purpose of the committee is [write a one- or two-line summary].

2. Membership and attendance

The committee shall comprise [insert number] members, including the committee chair. Members of the committee shall be appointed by the board. The board shall appoint the committee chair.

Only members of the committee have the right to attend committee meetings. However, other individuals such as [insert job title or name] may be invited to attend all or part of any meeting as and when appropriate and necessary.

Appointments to the committee shall be for a period of up to [insert number] years, which may be extended for further periods of up to [insert number] years, provided the board member still meets the criteria for membership of the committee.

3. Secretary

The board secretary or their nominee shall act as the secretary of the committee. They shall be responsible for ensuring that the committee is provided with appropriate support to take minutes of the meeting, collate and circulate papers, and ensure follow-up actions are delivered. Duties in this respect will include:

- agreement of the agenda with the chair and attendees, and collation of papers;
- taking the minutes and keeping a record of matters arising and issues to be carried forward;
- advising the committee on pertinent areas.

4. Quorum

The quorum necessary for the transaction of business shall be [insert number] members.

5. Meetings

5.1. The committee shall meet at least [insert number] times a year.

5.2. Meetings of the committee shall be called by the secretary of the committee at the request of any of its members if they consider it necessary.

5.3. Unless urgency necessitates a shorter notice period, notice of each meeting shall be given to each member of the committee no later than five working days before the date of the meeting.

5.4. The committee shall have the ability to hold meetings by suitable electronic means agreed by the committee in which each participant may communicate with all the other participants.

6. Functions

[*In this section, list the functions of the committee. The functions listed should be clear and comprehensive, as if something is not listed in this section it is outside the terms of reference of the committee and so should not be considered by it.*]

7. Accountability and reporting

7.1. The committee is accountable to the board and operates as a committee of it.

7.2. The committee will report to the board through update reports to each formal meeting and through an annual report.

7.3. The minutes of committee meetings shall be provided to board members.

8. Authority

The committee is authorised by the board to [*insert information*].

or

The committee shall be advisory only.

Outcomes and actions

This chapter gives an overview of the concept of governance and its importance for all organisations. It outlines some key things to consider when looking at your own governance framework. As a next step, you could look into adopting a governance code, if your organisation has not done so already. The chapter lists a number of available codes of governance. It might be a good idea to identify one that could be of relevance to your organisation, and then discuss its possible application and adoption with your board.

Checklists and examples

This section contains a number of checklists and examples that you may find useful in your role as secretary.

- Each **checklist** contains a number of important points for you to consider.
- Each **example** is a model format for suggestions that have been made throughout the book.

Checklist 1: on appointment as board secretary

Action	Notes	Checkmark
Check the constitution of the organisation – does it refer to a secretary? If so, does it state how they will be appointed and have you been appointed in accordance with those provisions?		
Have you been appointed by the board?	*The secretary should normally be appointed by the board. Even if you hold another position with acting as the secretary in its job description, there should still be a board minute stating that you have been appointed.*	
Has the previous secretary stood down or been removed and if so has this been recorded?	*This should be recorded in the register if one is held, or at Companies House if your organisation is a company.*	
Have you entered your name and details onto the register of secretaries (if your organisation should hold one)?		
If your organisation is a company, have you filed your details at Companies House?	*This should be done within 14 days of your appointment.*	
Do you have a role description setting out what you must do as secretary?	*Even if you hold another position and acting as secretary is a part of it, you should still have a role description for this part of your job.*	
Do you have a clear reporting line through to the board?	*Even if you hold another position and report to a manager or the chief executive in that capacity, you should have two reporting lines: for your other role and for the role of secretary.*	

Action	Notes	Checkmark
Do you have access to the meetings and information that you require to undertake the role?		
Do you need further training in the duties of being a secretary to undertake the role?		

Checklist 2: things to understand following your appointment as secretary

Action	Notes	Checkmark
Do you understand what legal form your organisation takes and what law applies?		
Is your organisation a charity?		
Have you located the current constitution and read it?	*Check that this is the version that is held by any regulators, such as the Charity Commission or Companies House.*	
Do you have a clear idea who your board members are?		
Do you know your board members' appointment dates and when their current terms of office end?		
Is your organisation a membership organisation? If so, find out who your members are (in the legal sense).	*Certain legal forms must have members, even if they are the same people as the board members.*	
Does your organisation have to hold registers? If so, can you locate them and are they up to date?		
Do you understand how your organisation is regulated?	*This will depend on its legal form.*	
Have you checked the information held by any regulators to see whether it is accurate and up to date? In other words, does it have the correct board members listed?		

Action	Notes	Checkmark
Do your organisation's accounts need to be filed? If so, when and with whom?		
Does your organisation have to complete an annual return? If so, when and with whom? And is the organisation up to date on this?		
If yours is a membership organisation, have you checked your constitution to see whether an AGM needs to be held? Is the organisation up to date on this?		
Do you know when your next board meeting is and what you need to do to prepare for it?		
Have you located and read through the papers of previous board meetings and the minutes of the last three board meetings?	*This should give you an idea of the work of the board, key themes and future agenda items.*	
Is the organisation meeting its legal requirements with regard to display of name and the information that it needs to provide on stationery (including your website)?	*This will depend on its legal form.*	
Do you have a clear understanding of which laws and regulatory requirements apply to your organisation? Even if you are not responsible for all of these, do you know who is and are you confident that they understand their responsibilities?		

Action	Notes	Checkmark
Does the organisation have any governance documents other than its constitution (such as standing orders, terms of office for committees or schedules of delegation)?	*Make sure that you locate and read the most up-to-date copies of these.*	
If your organisation has committees, are you clear about their next meetings and who is responsible for the administration of those committees?		
Do board members complete declarations of interest? Is there a register of interests and is it up to date?		
Has your organisation adopted a code of governance? If so, is it complying with the code and is there clarity about any areas of non-compliance?		

Checklist 3: how to identify whether your organisation is a charity

Note: this checklist provides a summary only, some additional guidance or advice may be necessary. It also only applies to charities in England and Wales.

Action	Notes	Checkmark
What legal form does your organisation take?	*If it is a charitable incorporated organisation, you will be a charity. If it is a community interest company, you cannot be a charity.*	
Is your organisation listed on the register of charities held by the Charity Commission?		
Is your organisation one of the types of organisation that is exempt or excepted from Charity Commission registration?	*Make sure to read and fully understand the Charity Commission's guidance on excepted charities, www.gov.uk/government/publications/excepted-charities/excepted-charities–2 (this guidance explains which charities are excepted and gives points of contact and links to relevant legislation); and on exempt charities (this guidance lists charities that are exempt from registration and regulation by the Charity Commission) www.gov.uk/government/publications/exempt-charities-cc23.*	
Has your organisation received acknowledgement from HMRC that it is charitable?		
Do you have charitable purposes? Do you have a non-distribution clause in your constitution? Are you established in England and Wales?	*Check your constitution. If all of these apply, your organisation is very likely to be a charity. You will need to register with the Charity Commission if you are not an exempt or excepted charity and if your income is more that £5,000 per year.*	

Checklist 4: on appointing a board member

Action	Notes	Checkmark
Has the board member been appointed in accordance with the proper processes?	*Check the constitution of your organisation. It will usually set out the processes for the appointment of board members.*	
Does the new board member meet the eligibility criteria?	*The constitution will also usually set out eligibility criteria for an appointment.*	
Does the new board member meet the legislative criteria for appointment as a board member for your type of organisation?	*For example, there are certain criteria for appointment as a company director.*	
Has the board member signed a statement confirming that they are eligible for the appointment and that they accept the appointment and the duties?	*If your organisation is a charity, this statement should meet the requirements of the HMRC in its fit and proper persons test.*	
Have you carried out checks regarding the board member's eligibility?	*You can carry out a check on the register of disqualified company directors and the insolvency register online. If your board member will come into contact with children or vulnerable adults, you should also consider whether further checks are necessary.*	
Is there clarity regarding the term of the appointment?		
Has the new board member been asked to complete a declaration of interests?		
Have you entered the new board member's name and details onto a register of board members (if your organisation should hold one)?		

Action	Notes	Checkmark
If your organisation is a company, have you filed the new board member's details at Companies House?	*This should be done within 14 days of their appointment.*	
Do you have a role description for board members? Has this been provided to the new board member?		
Have you arranged an induction for the new board member?		

Example 1: board member induction checklist

	Actioned by whom	Date actioned
Immediately on appointment		
Provide: • papers and minutes for the last three board meetings • constitution • strategy and business plan • budget • board members' contact details • key policies		
Set a date for a meeting with the chief executive (if applicable)		
Set a date for a meeting with the chair		
Within four weeks		
Meetings with the chief executive and chair should be held within four weeks, if possible. Issues to be covered should include: • history of the organisation • governance and staff structure • role of the board and board member • current strategy • key issues facing the organisation • financial position and funding • identifying specific skills of the new board member • any questions the new board member has • training and support needs for the new board member At least one meeting should be held at the main office if possible.		
Introduce the key staff if meetings are held at offices.		
Within eight weeks		
If the new board member has identified training or support needs, or a need for further information, provide outline proposals to the board member on how these will be addressed.		

	Actioned by whom	Date actioned
Within three months		
Arrange a follow-up meeting with the chair to allow the board member to give feedback, register problems and seek further information.		
Within four months		
If the new board member identified outstanding issues at the follow-up meeting, provide outline proposals to the board member on how these will be addressed.		
If any training or support needs have been identified, arrangements should have been made to address these by now.		
At the first board meeting following the appointment, give the new board member an opportunity to meet, prior to the meeting, with a member of staff to discuss the papers (usually earlier the same day). The aim of this meeting is to help the board member to catch up with ongoing issues by asking questions on the background to issues, decisions previously taken, jargon used and so on. It can also be useful to give the new board member an opportunity at this meeting to test out any questions or points they may want to raise (people are sometimes nervous about contributing to their first meeting). Note: this is an opportunity to test questions or points only. The issue should not be dealt with at the pre-meeting.		
Also at the first board meeting, introduce all board members (if this has not already happened). If possible, arrange more time for mixing either before or after the meeting (e.g. if the meeting begins with a buffet, ask the board members to arrive half an hour before the meeting to meet the new board member).		

Example 2: board member skills and experience analysis

Name: Date:

Occupation: Qualifications:

County:

Skills and experience (these should be specific to the organisation)	How this skill could have been obtained	Please rate your skill level from 1 (low) to 10 (high)	Give details of the nature/ source of your skills and experience (in other words, which of the bullet points in column two have been achieved, and how?)
Working in a group	• experience of working within an environment that encourages debate and discussion in order to reach collective decisions • membership of a group with decision-making powers • experience working in multi-disciplinary teams		
Strategic decision-making	• membership of a strategic board in an executive or non-executive capacity • experience of strategic decision-making in a dynamic environment • experience of working in an environment where a pragmatic and practical approach is required • experience of having to explain criteria for decisions made and to behave consistently • experience of trend analysis to predict future scenarios		

Skills and experience (these should be specific to the organisation)	How this skill could have been obtained	Please rate your skill level from 1 (low) to 10 (high)	Give details of the nature/ source of your skills and experience (in other words, which of the bullet points in column two have been achieved, and how?)
Governance	• member of a board • member of the organising committee of another organisation (e.g. a charity or voluntary group) • member of a governance committee at work		
Knowledge of the organisation	• involvement with a committee • involvement with a region • acting as a volunteer • experience of the organisation's work		
Finance	• member of a board • member of a finance committee • financial work experience • financial qualification • budget-holder at work • treasurer of an organisation or group		

Are there any particular areas where you feel you require further information, training or support?

_____

Please return to the Secretary by [*insert date of deadline*]

Checklist 5: preparing for a board meeting

Action	Notes	Checkmark
Are all attendees aware of the date of the meeting?		
Have a room or venue and catering (if required) been booked for the meeting?		
Have you drafted the agenda?	*It is usually a good idea to draft the agenda at least one month before the meeting. If there is an annual work programme for the board setting out which items it should be considering and when, you should use this as the basis for the draft agenda.* *Also check through the previous minutes to see whether any items were due to be considered by the board at this meeting. Use these sources and other information to create a first draft of the agenda.*	
Have you shared the draft agenda with the lead officer of the board (usually the chief executive if there is one) and the board chair?	*They should both approve a final draft.*	
Have you circulated the agenda to those people who will be expected to write papers for the meeting, and have you given them a clear deadline for submission of papers?	*Different organisations have different rules on the dispatch of papers prior to a meeting, but it is common for this to be done one week before the meeting, and it should not be done later than that. Ideally you will want papers submitted to you at least one day before you need to dispatch them, so that you can check them through.*	

Action	Notes	Checkmark
Have you proofread all of the papers that have come to you?	*The main things to consider are whether they are clear, whether they are of an appropriate length and whether they contain all of the information that the board will require to make a decision.* *You also need to ensure that there is clarity about what the board is expected to do with each paper – is it for information only, or are there recommendations to be considered? Are those recommendations clear?*	
Have you checked through the minutes of the previous meeting for actions that have been taken on them?	*It is a good idea to have a summary schedule completed that sets out what actions have been taken and what is still outstanding. This can shorten discussion on matters arising from the minutes.*	
Have you pulled together the final agenda, minutes of the previous meeting, the schedule of matters arising and any papers? Have you then dispatched them to the board members in accordance with your organisation's process?	*This should be done no later than one week before the meeting.*	
Have you asked board members to notify you in advance if they are not able to attend?		
Have you worked out the approximate timings for each agenda item and shared this with the lead officer and chair?	*Some organisations show the timings for agenda items on the agenda itself. Ensure that there is clarity and agreement as to how long should be allocated to each agenda item.*	

Action	Notes	Checkmark
Have you ensured that anyone presenting papers is clear as to how long has been allocated for their agenda item and how long their presentation (if required) should be?		
Have you allocated time for breaks in the meeting?	*Generally, a meeting should not run for more than 90 minutes without a break.*	
Will you provide briefing notes to the chair a few days before the meeting?	*Some organisations provide briefing notes for the chair of the meeting – sometimes called a chair's agenda. These can just be summary notes of who is leading on each agenda item, the time allocated, any potential conflicts of interest and a summary of what the board is being asked to agree.*	
Can you ensure that you arrive early to ensure that the venue or meeting room is set up properly?	*If audiovisual equipment is required (for presentations), ensure that it is working. If a telephone or video link is required, ensure that it is working. At the meeting itself, it is good practice for the lead officer (the chief executive) to sit on one side of the chair and the secretary to sit on the other side, to advise during the meeting as necessary.*	

Example 3: format of board agenda

Set out in this example is a format for a board agenda, with notes on each item. When you are drafting an agenda, it is a very good idea to consult the annual work programme for the board, which should set out what it will consider and when. You can then use this as a basis for each agenda. You should also try to draft the agenda in a way that means that the board will not lose sight of the principle of agenda integrity (i.e. that it will consider all of the items listed on the agenda, and only those items listed on the agenda).

A meeting should consider all of the items on its agenda and should not consider any items that are not on the agenda. This means that the agenda needs to be comprehensive but not overly long. There is a limit to how many different agenda items a board can take – no matter how long the meeting. Other than standard items (such as apologies, minutes of the last meeting and any other business), a good agenda should be no more than eight items long – including decisions, substantive agenda items and items for information. You may find this very difficult to achieve.

One last point to consider is that you should try to limit the use of board meetings for giving information to the board. A board's primary purpose is as a collective decision-making body. Board members are a key resource for your organisation and one that you will have limited use of – so do not waste time when your board members come together by just giving them information. Providing a regular information pack is one way of keeping the task of informing the board separate from their own meetings. Focus on agenda items that require discussion and decisions.

1 **Chair's introduction and welcome:** Not necessary on an agenda but some organisations like to start in this way and to have it listed as an agenda item.
2 **Apologies for absence:** This agenda item will be a verbal update on those board members who have sent their apologies. If a board member is not present but has not sent apologies or explained why they are not present, they should not be recorded as having sent apologies. You can record their non-attendance if you wish, but not their apologies. Likewise, while you may notify the board of any key staff or advisers who would usually attend at this point in the meeting,

they should not be included in the list of apologies received as they are not members of the board.

3 **Declarations of interest:** It is good practice to start each meeting by asking for any declarations of interest and for this to be an agenda item. If your board has a register of interests, it is sufficient to simply circulate a summary of this and then record that any interests on it were noted. This can prevent standing conflicts of interests having to be repeated at each meeting. Note, however, that recording any conflicts of interest at this point is different from the need for the board member to withdraw from the meeting when the relevant item is discussed, and it does not remove any requirement for them to do so.

4 **Minutes of the previous meeting:** This item is purely concerned with whether the minutes are approved and is different from discussion on matters arising, which should be separated out and discussed as the next item.

5 **Matters arising:** This agenda item is concerned with updating board members on actions taken on matters arising from the minutes which are not covered elsewhere on the agenda. It is a good idea to have a summary schedule that goes out with the agenda and papers, setting out what actions have been taken and what is still outstanding. This can shorten discussion on matters arising from the minutes. Some organisations get bogged down in this agenda item. Sometimes a board will spend far too long going through the previous minutes and discussing what has happened on each item. Even in some small organisations, the board does not have an agenda as such for its meetings – it just works its way through the previous minutes. If your board is spending too much time on this agenda item, then you should discuss alternatives with the board members. There is no real need to discuss matters arising at each meeting, although it is the usual practice. You could remove it as an agenda item altogether and just send out a summary of actions taken to board members (separate from the meeting).

6 **Smaller agenda items:** These are for scene-setting. The agenda now moves on to the main items and you need to think about how these should be structured. Best practice for meetings suggests that the agenda should follow a bell curve, with the most important decisions being taken in the middle of the meeting. This also links in with a principle called the 'two-thirds rule'. According to this rule, the first third of the meeting concerns any announcements and easy decisions, then the meeting moves on to more substantive decisions, and the final third of the meeting is rounded off with easy items (or

items that are for information only). Therefore, the first part of the agenda is the place for fairly straightforward decisions that need to be made, such as committee appointments. The two-thirds rule is based on the principle that participants are more mentally alert when they have settled into the meeting but that this alertness will decrease after a period. The bell curve principle works well, with two caveats.

6.1 Firstly, you may have some agenda items that need to be considered before others or that are part of the scene-setting for later decisions. If your chief executive provides a regular report on what is going on in the organisation and in the external environment, it might be useful to consider this first. On some occasions, considering information items such as this may be a way to provide context for the upcoming bigger decisions.

6.2 The second caveat is that the practice of always considering the same items at the end of the meeting may lead to insufficient time being allocated to it.

7 **Substantive agenda items:** The board now moves on to considering any substantive agenda items. It is my experience that it is nearly impossible for boards to make more than two substantive decisions at a meeting, and in many instances only one. If you try to squeeze more key decisions into a meeting, you may find that you end up with poor decisions that do not stand the test of time, or items may be deferred. If you want the board to make more than one key decision, make sure that the topics are in very different areas. In this way, board members' minds can stop their focus on one area and then shift to something completely different. These agenda items will usually have a large amount of time allocated to them (often about 30 minutes each). If there are any agenda items where it is helpful for the board to receive a short presentation in addition to the supporting papers, it will be these. Do remind lead officers and authors that the key point of these agenda items is discussion by the board, and not their presentation. The papers sent out in advance should give sufficient information and presentations should be kept short.

8 **Information items:** Bear in mind the previous point about limiting information items on the agenda. Having said that, the board will need to receive some monitoring information (such as on finance or performance), and this is typically dealt with in the third part of the agenda. This works well as these items should require less mental exertion, with no real decisions. However, it also needs to be remembered that this structure only works if sufficient time is left for this part of the agenda. If the agenda is too long or timings have not been allocated correctly, you may find that you begin to run out of time for this section and that these reports are dealt with in a very rushed way. Over time, this may mean that your board is not giving enough focus to its monitoring. If this is the case in your organisation, and you cannot shorten the agenda or deal with the timings better, it may be a good idea for you to re-order the agenda from time to time, to focus on these items at the start of the meeting so as to allow fuller consideration to be given to them.

9 **Any other business (AOB):** Most organisations have this as the last item of business. There needs to be clarity as to what this agenda item is for. It should essentially just be used for short items of information to be given to the board, or shared by board members, that were too late to go on the agenda. However, it is not good practice for AOB to be used for items requiring a decision, as board members will not have received notice of these items. If a matter does arise after the agenda has been sent out and it requires a decision by the board, the agenda should be revised and recirculated with that agenda item added onto it.

10 **Reflection on the meeting:** Some boards end each meeting with a short circuit around the table asking participants for their views on the meeting – what worked well and what did not.

11 **Date of next meeting:** Even if you have an annual programme of meetings, it is a good idea to list the date of the next meeting on the agenda, so that you can ensure that there is clarity and agreement.

Example 4: board meeting agenda

[*date and time of meeting*]

[*location of meeting*]

Time	Agenda item	Lead	Action required	Paper?
16.00	Apologies	Chair		
16.00	Declarations of interest	Chair/ Secretary	Consider	Yes
16.10	Minutes of meeting held on [*date of previous meeting*]	Chair	Approve	Yes
16.15	Matters arising	Secretary	Consider	Yes
16.20	Convening of AGM	Secretary	Approve	Yes
16.30	Committee appointments	Secretary	Approve	Yes
16.40	Annual business plan and budget	Chief Executive/ Head of Finance	Approve	Yes
17.10	Coffee break			
17.30	Review of grants policy	Head of Grants	Approve	Yes
18.00	KPIs and management accounts	Chief Executive/ Head of Finance	Consider	Yes
18.20	Any other business	Chair		
18.25	Appraisal of meeting			
	Date of next meeting: [*date and time*]			

Example 5: board work programme

	March	June	September	December
Standing items				
Chief executive report	✔	✔	✔	✔
Audit committee minutes	✔	✔	✔	✔
Performance report	✔	✔	✔	✔
Management accounts	✔	✔	✔	✔
Periodic items				
Annual report and accounts			✔	
Strategic review		✔		✔
Plan and budget	✔			
Remuneration committee	✔		✔	
Risk appetite				✔
Chief executive appraisal	✔			
Risk register		✔		✔
Meeting calendar			✔	
Items arising from minutes				
Governance review		✔		
Performance-related pay			✔	

Example 6: action summary

Previous meeting: [*date*]

Completed items in *italics*.

Meeting date	Action agreed	Action undertaken	Lead	Target date	Revised date
17 Oct. 2018	*Revisions to strategic objectives to be fed into the business plan for 2018–2019.*	*On agenda.*	*Chief executive*	*Mar-19*	
17 Oct. 2018	Propose amendments to the articles, to be taken to the AGM in July.	Much of the work has been undertaken. However, it is expected that there will be a revised set of model articles available in April. This will be awaited to see whether there is advised wording to be included, and then the Articles will be brought back to the board in May.	Secretary	Jan-19	May-19
12 Dec. 2018	Revise the format of the risk register and bring a revised policy to the board.	This work was delayed due to the resignation of the Head of Finance. The post has now been filled and this matter is being taken forward. The risk register and policy will be brought to the next board meeting.	Head of Finance	Mar-19	May-19
23 Jan. 2019	*Bring forward recommendations on committee appointments.*	*On agenda.*	*Secretary*	*Mar-19*	

Meeting date	Action agreed	Action undertaken	Lead	Target date	Revised date
23 Jan. 2019	A number of concerns were raised on the grants policy and it was agreed that this would be revised at the next meeting.	On agenda.	Head of Grants	Mar-19	
23 Jan. 2019	Purchase of 39 The High Street agreed, and chief executive given delegated power to purchase at price of up to £450,000.	Final sale price agreed at £430,000 and contracts have been exchanged. Completion to be reported to the next meeting.	Chief executive	Mar-19	

Checklist 6: effective meetings

Item	Checkmark
Does your board understand its role?	
Do you have an annual work programme for the board?	
Are meeting agendas focused on the core work of the board?	
Are board dates set well in advance (e.g. as part of an annual cycle)?	
Do you have sufficient time allocated to each meeting?	
Is the board agenda short enough?	
Do you have clarity on the timings for each agenda item?	
Does everyone understand their roles in the meeting?	
Does your board maintain agenda integrity?	
Are papers distributed far enough in advance?	
Are papers clear and concise?	
Are your meetings effectively chaired?	
Do all board members contribute to discussions?	
Are board meetings held in a way that encourages constructive challenge?	

Checklist 7: good governance regarding board size and composition

Item	Checkmark
Is your board a size that enables effective working?	
Is there clarity about terms of office?	
Is there a maximum term of office for board members?	
Is there a transparent and open process for the appointment of board members?	
Does the board have an understanding of what skills and competencies it needs its board members to have, and what gaps it has?	
Does the board undertake succession planning? Does it know what vacancies are likely to occur and why?	
If other bodies have a right to nominate onto your board, is this done on the basis of your needs in terms of skills and competency? If so, is there an understanding that board members cannot act as representatives?	

Useful addresses

Charity registration

Charity Commission for England and Wales

Charity Commission, PO Box 211, Bootle L20 7YX

Tel: 0300 066 9197; website: www.charity-commission.gov.uk

Charity Commission for Northern Ireland

267 Lough Road, Lurgon, Craigavon, Northern Ireland BT66 6NQ

Tel: 028 3832 0220; email: admin@charitycommissionni.org.uk;
website: www.charitycommissionni.org.uk

Office of the Scottish Charity Regulator (OSCR)

2nd Floor, Quadrant House, 9 Riverside Drive, Dundee DD1 4NY

Tel: 01382 220446; email: info@oscr.org.uk; website: www.oscr.org.uk

Charity law

Charity Law Association

PO Box 828, Gillingham ME8 1DJ

Tel: 01634 373253; email: admin@charitylawassociation.org.uk;
website: www.charitylawassociation.org.uk

Charity Tribunal

The First-tier Tribunal (Charity) Manager, Tribunals Operational Support
Centre, PO Box 9300, Leicester LE1 8DJ

Tel: 0300 123 4504

Community interest companies

The Office of the Regulator of Community Interest Companies

Room 3.68, Companies House, Crown Way, Maindy, Cardiff CF14 3UZ

Tel: 029 2034 6228 (24-hr voicemail service);
email: cicregulator@companieshouse.gov.uk

Company law

Companies House

England and Wales: Companies House, Crown Way, Cardiff CF14 3UZ

Tel: 0303 1234 500; email: enquiries@companies-house.gov.uk; website: www.companieshouse.gov.uk

London: Companies House, 4 Abbey Orchard Street, Westminster, London SW1P 2HT

Scotland: Companies House, 4th Floor Edinburgh Quay 2, 139 Fountainbridge, Edinburgh EH3 9FF

Northern Ireland: Second Floor, The Linenhall, 32–38 Linenhall Street, Belfast BT2 8BG

Equal opportunities

Equality and Human Rights Commission

London: Fleetbank House, 2–6 Salisbury Square, London EC4Y 8JX

Tel: 020 7832 7800 (non-helpline calls only);
email: info@equalityhumanrights.com

Manchester: Arndale House, The Arndale Centre, Manchester M4 3AQ

Tel: 0161 829 8100 (non-helpline calls only);
email: info@equalityhumanrights.com

Cardiff: Block 1, Spur D, Government Buildings, St Agnes Road, Gabalfa, Cardiff CF14 4YJ

Tel: 02920 447710 (non-helpline calls only);
email: wales@equalityhumanrights.com

Glasgow: 151 West George Street, Glasgow G2 2JJ

Tel: 0141 228 5910 (non-helpline calls only);
email: scotland@equalityhumanrights.com;
website: www.equalityhumanrights.com

Equality Advisory and Support Service

FREEPOST EASS HELPLINE FPN6521

Tel: 0808 800 0082; Textphone: 0808 800 0084;
website: www.equalityadvisoryservice.com

Finance
Charity Bank

Headquarters, Fosse House, 182 High Street, Tonbridge, Kent TN9 1BE

Tel: 01732 7441900; email: enquiries@charitybank.org

All deposit account applications should be sent to the Headquarters.

If you would like to discuss a loan requirement, call directly on 01732 441919 or send an email to enquiries@charitybank.org.

Financial Conduct Authority

25 The North Colonnade, Canary Wharf, London E14 5HS

Tel: 0800 111 6768; website: www.fsa.org.uk

Fundraising
Institute of Fundraising

Charter House, 13–15 Carteret Street, London SW1H 9DJ

Tel: 020 7840 1000; email: info@institute-of-fundraising.org.uk; website: www.institute-of-fundraising.org.uk

See the Institute of Fundraising website for information on fundraising codes of practice.

Fundraising Regulator

2nd floor, CAN Mezzanine Building, 49–51 East Road, London N1 6AH

Tel: 0300 999 3407; email: enquiries@fundraisingregulator.org.uk; website: www.fundraisingregulator.org.uk

Governance
ICSA: The Governance Institute

Saffron House, 6–10 Kirby Street, London EC1N 8TS

Tel: 020 7580 4741; email: info@icsa.org.uk; website: www.icsa.org.uk/knowledge/charity-resources, www.icsa.org.uk

Housing associations
National Housing Federation (NHF)

Lion Court, 25 Procter Street, London WC1V 6NY

Tel: 020 7067 1010; email: info@housing.org.uk; website: www.housing.org.uk

Information and training for the voluntary and community sector

Directory of Social Change

London office: 352 Holloway Road, London N7 6PA

Tel: 020 7697 4200; email: cs@dsc.org.uk; website: www.dsc.org.uk

Liverpool office: Suite 103, 1 Old Hall Street, Liverpool L3 9HG; email: research@dsc.org.uk

See page 205 onwards for publications available from DSC.

Local organisations

Councils for voluntary service (CVS) and rural community councils (RCCs) are registered charities that support local organisations in their area (CVS tend to work in towns and cities, RCCs in more rural areas).

For information on your local CVS, contact: National Association for Voluntary and Community Action, Floor 2, Churchill House, 6–8 Meetinghouse Lane, Sheffield S1 2DP

Tel: 0114 278 6636; email: navca@navca.org.uk; website: www.navca.org.uk

For information on your nearest RCC, contact: Action with Communities in Rural England (ACRE), Suite 109, Unit 9, Cirencester Office Park, Tetbury Road, Cirencester GL7 1TW

Tel: 01285 653477; email: acre@acre.org.uk; website: www.acre.org.uk

National organisations

England

National Council for Voluntary Organisations, Society Building, 8 All Saints Street, London N1 9RL

Tel: 020 7713 6161; email: ncvo@ncvo.org.uk; website: www.ncvo-vol.org.uk

Northern Ireland

Northern Ireland Council for Voluntary Action, 61 Duncairn Gardens, Belfast BT15 2GB

Tel: 028 9087 7777; email: info@nivca.org; website: www.nicva.org

Scotland

Scottish Council for Voluntary Organisations, Mansfield Traquair Centre, 15 Mansfield Place, Edinburgh EH3 6BB

Tel: 0131 474 8000; email: enquiries@scvo.org.uk; website: www.scvo.org.uk

Wales

Wales Council for Voluntary Action, Baltic House, Mount Stuart Square, Cardiff CF10 5FH

Tel: 0800 2888 329; email: help@wcva.org.uk; website: www.wcva.org.uk

UK-wide

Association of Chief Executives of Voluntary Organisations (ACEVO), Regent's Wharf, 8 All Saints Street, London N1 9RL

Tel: 020 7014 4600; email: info@acevo.org.uk; website: www.acevo.org.uk

Sources of funding

Awards for All (Big Lottery Fund)

Within the Big Lottery Fund there is a small grants scheme which is sometimes referred to as Awards for All. It exists across various areas of the UK.

England

For projects where the beneficiaries are based in the Eastern, North East, North West, South East or Yorkshire and the Humber regions, contact:

Big Awards for All, 2 St James' Gate, Newcastle upon Tyne NE1 4BE

Tel: 0845 410 2030; email: general.enquiries@awardsforall.org.uk

For projects where the beneficiaries are based in the East Midlands, West Midlands, London or South West regions contact:

Big Awards for All, Apex House 3 Embassy Drive Calthorpe Road, Edgbaston, Birmingham B15 1TR

Tel: 0845 410 2030; email: general.enquiries@awardsforall.org.uk

Northern Ireland

Big Lottery Fund, 1 Cromac Quay, Cromac Wood, Ormeau Road, Belfast BT7 2JD

Tel: 028 9055 1455; email: enquiries.ni@biglotteryfund.org.uk

Scotland

Big Lottery Fund, Pacific House, 70 Wellington Street, Glasgow G2 6UA

Tel: 0300 123 7110; email: enquiries.scotland@biglotteryfund.org.uk

Wales

Big Lottery Fund, 10th Floor, Helmont House, Churchill Way, Cardiff CF10 2DY

Tel: 0300 123 0735; email: enquiries.wales@biglotteryfund.org.uk

Tax and giving

HMRC Charities

Charities, Savings and International 2, HM Revenue and Customs, Bootle BX9 1BU

Tel: 0300 123 1073 (charities helpline); email: charities@hmrc.gov.uk; website: www.gov.uk/charities-and-tax

HMRC provides information and advice about the taxation of charities, including VAT.

Charities Aid Foundation (CAF)

25 King's Hill Avenue, West Malling, Kent ME19 4TA

Tel: 03000 123000; email: enquiries@caf.charitynet.org; website: www.cafonline.org

CAF provides information about tax-effective giving.

Volunteering

National Council for Voluntary Organisations (NCVO)

Society Building, 8 All Saints Street, London N1 9RL

Tel: 020 7713 6161; email: ncvo@ncvo-vol.org.uk; website: www.ncvo.org.uk

NCVO provides advice and information on the law and best practice in volunteering.

Further reading

Publications

Some of these publications have been referred to earlier in this book, throughout the main text. Some of them have been published by DSC and others are from other print and online sources. It is recommended that you look into these for a better overall understanding of the sector and environment of the role of the board secretary in charity organisations.

Sarah Atkinson, 'The New Charity Governance Code – Essential reading for all trustees' [web article], Charity Commission, accessible at https://charitycommission.blog.gov.uk/2017/07/13/the-new-charity-governance-code-essential-reading-for-all-trustees, 13 July 2017.

Taken on Trust: The awareness and effectiveness of charity trustees in England and Wales [PDF], Cass Business School, The Charity Commission and the Worshipful Company of Management Consultants, London, The Charity Commission, 2017, accessible at https://www.gov.uk/government/publications/taken-on-trust-awareness-and-effectiveness-of-charity-trustees-in-england-and-wales.

Charity Commission Annual Report and Accounts 2016–17 [PDF], Charity Commission, 2017, accessible at www.gov.uk/government/uploads/system/uploads/attachment_data/file/628747/Charity_Commission_Annual_Report_and_Accounts_2016_17_web.pdf.

Tackling Abuse and Mismanagement 2016–17: Full report, Charity Commission, 2018, accessible at www.gov.uk/government/publications/tackling-abuse-and-mismanagement-2016-17/tackling-abuse-and-mismanagement-2016-17-full-report.

Charity Governance Code, 2018, accessible at www.charitygovernancecode.org; PDF versions of both the small and large charity editions are available from www.charitygovernancecode.org/en/pdf.

Memorandum and Articles of Association, 3rd edition, Charity Law Association, 2017.

The collapse of Kids Company: lessons for charity trustees, professional firms, the Charity Commission, and Whitehall [PDF], House of Commons Public Administration and Constitutional Affairs Committee, Fourth Report of Session 2015–16, 2016, accessible at https://publications.parliament.uk/pa/cm201516/cmselect/cmpubadm/433/433.pdf.

Andrew Kakabadse, Nada Korac-Kakabadse and Nadeem Khan, *The Company Secretary: Building trust through governance*, London, ICSA: The

Governance Institute, 2014. This publication is accessible to ICSA members at www.icsa.org.uk/knowledge/research/the-company-secretary-report; and to non-members at www.geniusmethods.com/wp-content/uploads/2015/01/icsa-the-company-secretary-report.pdf.

Sir Christopher Kelly, *Failings in management and governance: Report of the independent review into the events leading to the Co-operative Bank's capital shortfall* [PDF], 2014, accessible at https://assets.ctfassets.net/5ywmq66472jr/3LpckmtCnuWiuuuEM2qAsw/9bc99b1cd941261bca5d674724873deb/kelly-review.pdf.

Panorama Developments (Guildford) Ltd v Fidelis Furnishing Fabrics Ltd (1971), 2 QB, 711. Some further information on the case can be found at https://alchetron.com/Panorama-Developments-(Guildford)-Ltd-v-Fidelis-Furnishing-Fabrics-Ltd.

Regulating Charities: a landscape review [PDF], National Audit Office, 2012, accessible at www.nao.org.uk/wp-content/uploads/2012/07/Regulating_charities.pdf.

The Charities Act 2011, UK Government, 2011, accessible at www.legislation.gov.uk/ukpga/2011/25.

Companies Act 2006, UK Government, 2006, accessible at www.legislation.gov.uk/ukpga/2006/46/contents.

Charity Commission publications

The Charity Commission produces a range of free publications. The most generally useful titles (all available online) include:

CC3 – The essential trustee: what you need to know, what you need to do *and* The essential trustee: 6 main duties

CC3a – Charity trustee: what's involved

CC7 – Ex gratia payments by charities

CC8 – Internal financial controls for charities

CC9 – Campaigning and political activity guidance for charities

CC11 – Trustee expenses and payments

CC12 – Managing a charity's finances

CC14 – Charities and investment matters: a guide for trustees

CC15b – Charity reporting and accounting: the essentials

CC19 – Charity reserves: building resilience

CC20 – Charity fundraising: a guide to trustee duties

CC21a – How to set up a charity

CC21b – How to register a charity

CC22b – How to write your charity's governing document

CC24 – Users on board: beneficiaries who become trustees

CC27 – It's your decision: charity trustees and decision making

CC29 – Conflicts of interest: a guide for charity trustees

CC35 – Trustees trading and tax: how charities may lawfully trade

CC49 – Charities and insurance

GD1 – Charitable Companies: Model Articles of Association

GD2 – Charitable Trusts: Model Trust Deed

GD3 – Charitable Associations: Model Constitution

To see all the publications available, you can go to their website and find them accessibly listed in one place: www.gov.uk/government/organisations/charity-commission/about/publication-scheme.

See page 197 for contact details for the Charity Commission.

Publications available from DSC

The following is a selection of publications available from the Directory of Social Change, the leading publisher and provider of training for the voluntary sector. (See page 200 for contact details to request a complete list of current publications.)

Fundraising directories

There are thousands of trusts and foundations in the UK that give grants to charities and other voluntary organisations. However, their funding criteria differ – some only give money for certain specified causes; some only give in certain geographic areas – as does the information they require from applicants. To help you identify those trusts that may fund your particular cause, the following DSC directories give detailed information, including independent commentary, on the largest UK trusts.

The Directory of Grant Making Trusts

The Guide to Educational Grants

The Guide to Grants for Individuals in Need

The Guide to Major Trusts

The Guide to New Trusts

The Guide to UK Company Giving

The data from the directories is also accessible online at DSC's subscription funding website, which you can find information on here: www.dsc.org.uk/funding-website.

Management and governance

Readers of this book who are becoming board secretaries may be interested in the following publications which cover governance issues. These are all available from DSC.

Debra Allcock Tyler, *It's Murder in Management*, London, DSC, 2018.

Debra Allcock Tyler, *It's Tough at the Top*, London, DSC, 2006 (reprinted 2017).

Mike Eastwood and Jacqueline Williams, *The Charity Trustee's Handbook*, 3rd edition, London, DSC, 2017.

Mike Hudson and Jacinta Ashworth, *Delivering Effective Governance*, London, DSC in association with Compass Partnership, 2012.

Mike Hudson, *Managing Without Profit*, 4th edition, London, DSC, 2017.

Mike Hudson, *One Minute Tips on Governance*, London, DSC in association with Compass Partnership and Third Sector, 2014.

Alan Lawrie, *Business and Strategic Planning for Voluntary Organisations*, 4th edition, London, DSC, 2014.

Steve McCurley, Rick Lynch and Rob Jackson, *The Complete Volunteer Management Handbook*, 3rd edition, London, DSC, 2012.

Steve McCurley and Rick Lynch, *Keeping Volunteers*, London, DSC, 2010 (reprinted 2016).

Fraser Dyer and Ursula Jost, *Recruiting Volunteers*, London, DSC, 2002 (reprinted 2013).

Finance

Gareth G. Morgan, *The Charity Treasurer's Handbook*, 5th edition, London, DSC, 2017.

Kate Sayer and Alastair Hardman, *The Complete Charity VAT Handbook*, 4th edition, London, DSC in association with Sayer Vincent, 2016.

Secretarial tasks

Moi Ali, *Speed Read: Writing for Work*, London, DSC, 2009.

Helen Rice and Maria Pemberton, *Speed Read: Meetings*, London, DSC, 2011.

Brian Rothwell, *Speed Read: Delegation*, London, DSC, 2009.

Paul Ticher and Lee Comer, *Key Guides: Minute Taking*, 2nd edition, London, DSC, 2012.

Index

What else can DSC do for you?

Let us help you to be the best you possibly can be. DSC equips individuals and organisations with expert skills and information to help them provide better services and outcomes for their beneficiaries. With the latest techniques, best practice and funding resources all brought to you by our team of experts, you will not only boost your income but also exceed your expectations.

dsc.org.uk/**cth**

dsc.org.uk/**cio**

dsc.org.uk/**ctr**

Publications
With over 75 titles, we produce fundraising directories and research reports, as well as accessible 'how to' guides and best practice handbooks, all to help you to help others.

Conferences and fairs
DSC conferences are a fantastic way to network with voluntary sector professionals while taking part in intensive, practical training workshops.

Training
The voluntary sector's best-selling training – we run over 300 courses per year covering all of the sector's needs.

Funding website
DSC's subscription funding website provides access to thousands of grant-making charities, statutory funding and corporate donations. You won't get more funders, commentary and analysis anywhere else. Find out more at **www.dsc.org.uk/funding-website**.

@DSC_Charity
For top tips and special offers

Visit our website today and see what we can do for you: www.**dsc.org.uk**

Or contact us directly: publications@dsc.org.uk